YOU'VE ARRIVED

A 5-Step System to Bypass Your Logical Mind, Activate Your Intuitive Potential and Gain Perfect Clarity in Your Business

Second Edition

Lynn M. Scheurell

#1 Bestselling Author

FREE – Bonus E-course

This book includes a 7-day e-course you can use RIGHT NOW to cut through the noise, distractions, and stories to gain clarity for your business decisions.

Get It NOW at
www.GEENISystem.com

MIZRAHI PRESS

Copyright ©2022 Creative Catalyst, LLC

Printed in the United States of America

No part of this publication may be reproduced, stored in a retrieval system or transmitted in any form by any means, electronic or mechanical, photocopying, recording, scanning or otherwise except as permitted under Section 107 or 108 of the 1976 United States Copyright Act, without the prior written permission of the Publisher.

ISBN-13: 978-0-9801550-8-2 (paperback)

Limit of Liability/Disclaimer of Warranty
While the author has used their best efforts in preparing this report, they make no representation or warranties with respect to the accuracy or completeness of the contents and specifically disclaim any implied warranties. The advice and strategies contained herein may not be suitable for your situation. You should consult with a professional where appropriate. The author shall not be liable for any loss of profit or any other commercial damages, including but not limited to special, incidental, consequential or other damages.

Published by Mizrahi Press
A Division of Creative Catalyst LLC
MyCreativeCatalyst.com

Table of Contents

Introduction: Welcome to GEENI!   1
    What to Expect in This Book   4

Endorsements and Accolades   7

Overview and Explanation of This Book   11
    When Do You Need GEENI?   16
    Who Am I and Why Should You Listen to or Trust Me?   20

The Secret Sauce: Your Perception   23
    The GEENI System Explained   26
    Defining GEENI   29
    A Word About Change   30
    How to Use GEENI   32
    Asking Quality Questions for Clarity   33

G Stands for Greater Truth   37
    Get Started with G Now   44
    A Personal G Story   47
    The Sacred Exchange   49

E Is for Energy   53

- Money Energy and the 7 Business Systems   55
- 2 Simple Shifts You Can Make Now   58
- 6 Myths Blocking People from Using Energy as a Guide   61

E Is for Environment   67

- About Your Feng Shui   70

N is Your Natural Intelligence   79

- 9 Secrets to Creating Positive Change Through Natural Intelligence   82
- Go Beyond Your Reason   86
- Naked Intelligence   91

I Stands for Integrity   97

- Integrity is the Glue for Sustainable Success   99
- The Language of Integrity   100
- It's a New Age   103

Summary and Next Steps   117

The People Who Get the Greatest Value from My Work   119

About Lynn Scheurell   123

Book Lynn Scheurell to Speak   125

Other Books by Lynn Scheurell   127

One Last Thing   129

Introduction: Welcome to GEENI!

How do we create our world? What are we here for? Why do we matter? People, including me, are rethinking their place in the world, along with their business / work goals.

Finding the answers to these questions and others has kept me busy for most of my adult life. The single pursuit of understanding how change works, how change affects us, and how we create or deny change fascinates me on every level. It is my purpose in life to discover and distill these huge questions and their answers into something that makes sense for others. After years of studying myself and other people (guru-types, clients, friends, associates, family, and anybody else who has breathed in my world), I have finally integrated what I know to be true into a system.

My prime directive in life is to facilitate and support people in activating their potential to create their most successful life—and to live it NOW—by their own definition. And that's a big statement. It incorporates not only personal knowingness with the ability to visualize, manifest, and enjoy in this third-dimension state of being, but also reference the universal laws of creation, attraction, and connection, among others. Given that our time here is brief, there is an implied sense of urgency.

Knowing what we want and giving ourselves the permission and resources to go after and actually have it is a big part of why we are here. We are part of a greater whole that is only served by us being our true selves. Us being anything less takes away from everybody and everything else. It's a little selfish to think we don't matter, that we don't add to the world around us. After all, it is because of us that our world IS.

I have come to that discovery after many bittersweet adventures—both my own and those of others. It might seem convoluted or counterintuitive in the initial awareness of it but, when we understand we ARE the power to create what we want, the world suddenly feels very different. Then, once we get that clarity, what do we *do* with it? And how do we begin the process of intentional change?

My intention is the following system will help you discover what you have created in your world and what is really happening for (not to) you. It's vital you understand more of who you are, and to create and live success by your own definition. This book is the sum of nearly 25 years of experience, hard work, and insights from my wonderful, visionary, and generous clients, friends, and colleagues.

This framework for bypassing the logical mind to access intuitive insights was born during an eight-hour drive when I was going to meet the world's small business guru. I mean, what do you say about what you do when you're going to meet Michael Gerber?

At that point, I had been in business for nearly a decade. I had worked with hundreds of people to help them sort out their situations, gain clarity, and be able to make new decisions around having more of their dreams in real time. My thought was to synthesize the themes

INTRODUCTION: WELCOME TO GEENI!

of what people grappled with through my work so I could identify patterns. Once I saw the patterns, my plan was to consolidate my work into a concise approach that described how I helped my clients understand their results and how to upgrade them through clear and simple insights. *The GEENI™ System that you see here is the result.*

All great accomplishment is preceded by profound quiet. From primitive hunters to global leaders, from tidal waves to avalanches, from solving a problem to stepping on to a stage for public performance, all great feats require a gathering of internal resources for clear outer expression.

At some point, you must go beyond the rational into your wisdom to captivate the power available in any opportunity. You might notice this need through a state of unexplainable restlessness or unease. That state of being requires an inner alchemy of insight, knowingness, and surrender to the greater flow for respite. The container of self must expand to accommodate a larger knowledge. And the state of wisdom becomes more than accumulated knowledge—it is your presence and ability to discern next-level perspective.

Fortunately, there is an emerging energy for people today to ride the wave of intrinsic motivation and express who they are at an essential level which often means through their own business. Most of my clients are, or want to be, in their own business. So, while I wrote this based on my tribe, this system works for anyone in any situation.

Essentially, it's not enough to be 'doing' anymore; now it's about inspiring and activating authentic power. In that profound space for awareness, it's about practicing discernment to interpret and then express wisdom. In doing so, one shapes perception, solves problems, meets needs and, ultimately, changes the world through their presence.

What to Expect in This Book

Here is what to expect in this book so you can get the most out of it.

First, it's practical. Great ideas are meaningless unless you know what to do with them. There are opportunities for you to go deeper into the content through access to free resources and join my online communities.

Second, this book is for business clarity. It's intended to help you activate your intuition for discernment so you can make next-level decisions and accelerate your results.

Third, it's for visionary action-takers. This system, like any other, will do nothing if you don't apply it. While this is written for people who want or have their own business, regardless of the location or type of business, anyone can benefit from it.

Note this is NOT a get-rich-quick scheme nor is it about hooking you into some big-box program. My intention is it gives you—the visionary action-taker—a new way to get fresh perspective that bypasses your logical, conditioned limitations so you can gain new levels of personal and professional achievement.

Fourth, this book wasn't intended to be a #1 Bestseller, although that is what happened. Instead, it is designed to start a narrative conversation so we can get to know each other a bit, develop trust, explore ideas and, ultimately, help us decide if we will work together someday.

Fifth, this book—while short—is a journey in self-mastery. The purpose of this book is to show you a revolutionary 5-part system that can help you understand the results you've been getting and how to upgrade them through clear, simple insights. Through alignment with your truth, your life and business can attract new opportunities, benefit through new strategies, and accelerate intentional results.

INTRODUCTION: WELCOME TO GEENI!

Personally, I am committed to helping you help more people through your business. And, in the interest of transparency, I do have programs that can continue our work together when it feels right for you to do so.

However, having said that, if you like what you get from this book, I would love to hear from you. I want to know you and your business. I would be honored to read your book 'takeaway' story on my Facebook wall at **facebook.com/MyCreativeCatalyst**.

Please visit the links you find in this book and join me in the resources on my site to begin our relationship together. It's an honor for me to be your Catalyst in having the life and business you really want so you can help more people, have more fulfillment, and enjoy more freedom every day.

> To your fresh perspective with GEENI,
> With good energy ~
> ~ Lynn

P.S.: If you enjoy this book or gain new clarity because of it, will you please post a short review on Amazon? If you'd like to leave a review, just visit this link: **GeeniBook.com**. Your support makes all the difference and I would be grateful. I read each review personally so I can learn and grow too. If you *don't* like it, send me an email, tell me why and I'll give you your money back.

Thanks again for your support. Here's to bypassing limitations and activating potential for fresh clarity and accelerated results.

Endorsements and Accolades

Lynn Scheurell and Client

"When I met Lynn, she told me that she was a catalyst for entrepreneurs. In other words, if you're looking to do something really, really, really fast—that's what she helps you do. What normally would happen in maybe a year or two or three suddenly happens in two, three, four days, maybe a week, cutting things down an enormous time. You taught me how to get a lot done in a very short time. You got my mind thinking in new parameters. Like a lightswitch. Catalyst. There was a 'before catalyst' curve and an 'after catalyst' curve. You showed me to ask: 'What's in here?' And then to take action on it!"

—Carl White, Entrepreneur

"Lynn, I have to say you are so the g-word—"guru" {def: guru}. As I see it, you use your light to help illuminate the light within others and you meet them where they are to do so, even when their bulbs are dim! Thank you for helping me change my life."

—Michelle Newbon, Content Manager

"Lynn has been a powerful influence in my personal and professional quest to develop a more conscious, balanced, sustainable way of being and knowing that I could apply to all aspects of my life. Studying with Lynn over the last four years, I have felt like a grad student soaking up applied knowledge with an attitude of curiosity, wonder and joy. I have learned how to take appropriate actions to bypass my own individual limitations and to clearly trust my internal guidance system in making the right choices. She has inspired me to, ultimately, be the master life gardener and designer of myself and showed me how to plant seeds of possibilities in the right environment to grow where I want go. With her guidance, I have become empowered and open to embrace possible change from a view of opportunity rather than with fear."

—dLee, Radio Show Host and Author

"If you are overwhelmed with too many great ideas, Lynn will help you determine where you should put your time, energy and resources. I went to her with an abundance of creative ideas and no time to pursue any of them. With Lynn's help, I've let go of some ideas, developed others and finally put a sensible strategy together to maximize not only my bottom-line profits, but my excitement for the projects I'm working on. The space Lynn provides and the timely insight she offers is priceless."

—Christine Kloser, Book Coach

"What amazes me is that Lynn has both the intuitive knowledge and the ability to extract the same from her clients by asking open and apparently non-dangerous questions so it feels safe it to answer them with our innermost intuitive responses. In fact, we open to our larger unconscious mind instead of only relying on previous experiences. This is where the deeper truth lies and where it is so difficult to get to because it sometimes defies all logic—but it is a fraction of what Lynn achieves through her work."

—Gitte Hegelund, Fortune 500 Project Manager

ENDORSEMENTS AND ACCOLADES

"In the billion-dollar plus business consulting industry, "experts" abound, and yet few of these gurus have what it takes to truly make a long lasting or permanent change in their client's lives and work. Lynn's understated manner and quiet confidence do not do justice to her passion in helping people realize their goals. She is a powerhouse of knowledge and useful information that she puts to work immediately. Lynn rises above the crowd in all areas. She truly lives what she teaches. She is practical, level-headed, honest, organized and committed. She goes beyond the expected, creating new ideas and new ways to implement them beyond what she promises. She is a true catalyst who takes a person's creative idea or talent and makes positive results happen."

—Bradley James, Composer

"Lynn is the most talented coach I have ever met. Many people claim they are mentors, but very few walk their talk and live their work, especially with the level of integrity and authenticity that Lynn does. Her listening skills are second to none; this coupled with her kind heart and savvy life skills makes her the one you want in your corner. Lynn mentors with heart and her head. She gives a bit of theory and a LOT of practical application so you not only get the why, you get the how—and that is a VERY rare combination in this world."

—Viki Viertel, Freelancer

"I expected to learn a few things to apply to my business to help me make some changes, what I received was so much more than that! Lynn is truly amazing. She helped me to see small and large changes that would make my business so much more effective. She used her intuition to say things in just the right way. She used her delightful loving presence to make me feel comfortable with every moment of our session. Working with her was a total pleasure and I learned more that I could have ever imagined. Lynn has changed my whole life and I highly recommend her and the amazing work that she does. Invest in yourself through Lynn Scheurell if you are ready to take your whole life to a higher level!"

—Barbara Grace, Healer

"Lynn Scheurell is one of the brilliant lights of this world. She is clearly passionate about helping. Her energy is uplifting and positive and she gives with free-flowing creativity. I would recommend her to anyone with a budding business, who wants to shift their consciousness into the new paradigm."

—M. Sareen, Herbalist

"Conventional coaches may say things but give no substance behind it—no motion, no connection to one's own energy of the moment/topic. They essentially are "human products", repeating recipes at people as if THEY know where that person needs to go. As the saying goes (paraphrased by Maslow, I believe), if the only tool in your toolbox is a hammer, everything looks like a nail. Which is 180 degrees from what you do. You have a full tool box and choose the appropriate tool for the job…and you change tools when necessary, as many times as it takes, as the nail turns into a screw becomes a staple. In general, people cannot even begin to comprehend what you actually do in following someone's energy and dancing with them, because it is so far outside the realm of the familiar and not even on people's radar as possible. What you offer is vastly different…despite plenty of searching and hearing some similar, or even identical words, people don't get what you offer…empowerment, feeling heard and responded to, not talked to or given advice or suggestions. You mirror one's highest self, one's best unshrouded energy around a topic so a person can grow. And the only way you can do that is to be ego-less and allow someone to see Source through you and to feel it in oneself. And the person is forever changed and charged, and differently responsible for oneself, regardless of what s/he chooses to do with the experience and shift afterward. There isn't a product in the world that does that. Another big difference about what you do is that you teach from where your "student" is, not from where you are. You rock. You are amazing. I am so, so, so honored to be here with you in this physical time and space experience. Namaste, in the truest, most non-cliche sense of that word."

—Carrie Mayes, Chiropractor

Overview and Explanation of This Book

What is GEENI and how will it change your business results?

Business is simple—essentially, it's an exchange of value. The customer buys a solution that meets a need or solves a problem which the merchant then delivers. It's everything else that makes business complicated.

The recent global shift due to the pandemic, and all its associated consequences that will leave social scars for many years, has surfaced two significant changes in business in general.

1. Business owners are struggling to hold onto the businesses they have and leverage their previous hard work.
2. People are discovering that maybe being in business for themselves creates a way to spread their wings and have "more" while working from home on their own terms.

It's easy to get caught up in the doing of your business. You've got multiple priorities (on probably more than one to-do list), constantly reacting to what's happening while being proactive at identifying and taking advantage of new opportunities, knowing your niche/message/product, measuring your success/expenses/revenues while you're marketing/delivering services/following up.

Then, at the same time, there's the strategy you need to develop and implement for future growth so you're working *on* your business while you're working *in* it.

As a result, you're likely working long hours because it usually takes more time than you think... or at least you're thinking about your business even when you're not working it directly and wishing you could be... and the whole time life is happening all around and through you. And yes, any greatness that's ever been achieved happens outside of typical working hours, and passion work doesn't feel like hard labor. At the same time, one of two things typically happens.

The net result of working so much goes one of two ways for entrepreneurs: 1) they personalize 'failure' as a character deficit and feel lost, overwhelmed, and stuck, or 2) they get frustrated because they are doing well but know they could be doing better and don't know how to make it happen. Actually, there is a third consequence—Insufficient Reward Syndrome, where brain chemistry is permanently altered.

According to *"Behavior Therapy in Dealing with Depression"* (June 2011, Volume 42, Issue 2), there are four factors that apply in a behavior to positive reinforcement ratio which influence whether you will experience this condition. The idea is you can predict behavior based on positive reinforcement (or lack of it). The four factors are:

- Frequency of positive rewards
- Amount of positive rewards
- The duration and continuation of the rewards once started
- The amount of effort required to produce expected behavior

In other words, if your rewards are infrequent, too conservative and/or prone to stopping even though the behavioral demands continue, you're going to suffer 'Insufficient Reward Syndrome.'

Even more, if the effort to perform increases, the behavior to reinforcement ratio also increases and, if not met, also results in a deficient rewards syndrome state. The bottom line is the quality of your life and health depends on your ability to reward yourself consistently in proportion to the effort you're putting out. It helps you to stay motivated and in joy.

That being said, as an entrepreneur, chances are you're focusing on your bottom line rather than your body when you're deciding whether to give yourself a reward like time off, a new toy or a frivolous expenditure. And when you *don't* reward yourself, you affect your biology, your ability to focus, your productivity, and your ability to reach your full potential. Rewards don't have to be expensive... but they are vital to your well-being.

Ironically, social conditioning for success teaches that we must finish our plate before we have dessert; that is, we have to fill up our schedule and our capacity with where we are now before we get to increase our fees, or make a current program successful before designing another. And yet, entrepreneurs must seize the opportunities as they present in order to take advantage of them while they're hot. If something isn't working, fail forward fast—it doesn't behoove you to work on a project that isn't producing.

The other issue here is entrepreneurs can think more about their clients than their own welfare with their pricing strategy. If you aren't charging enough to compensate you for the energy you are putting out to serve your clients, you will end up with a deficit energetically. You will feel drained, tired, and maybe even resentful of your clients. Charging less than you deserve is a disservice to everyone because you don't have 'the juice' to continue to serve your clients.

Let's get back to the subject at hand...how do you make the most of your business—and even enjoy it along the way? Because this is it—this isn't a dress rehearsal and you don't get today back. At the same time, your cup is already full...so what's a (wannabe) successful entrepreneur to do?

Every business owner is responsible for creating and sustaining the revenues that define having a successful business. Many times, that means to go beyond reason, to go with what you know vs. what you are told (or even believe).

To be a successful entrepreneur means:

- Going against the grain and 'zagging' when others are 'zigging' to do business *your* way.
- Knowing what you uniquely know and being willing to risk following it.
- Speaking your truth but only when necessary and in the right audience, as anything less only wastes your breath.
- Exploring the edge of your being with fresh perspective and a willingness to see what is unknown, unfamiliar and unexpected.
- Releasing what doesn't serve you *even* if you don't want to let go or are not sure of what else is waiting for you.

As an entrepreneur, it is unreasonable to live your life by someone else's definition. But it is counter-intuitive to be 'hard' and 'soft' at the same time—to set boundaries *and* still be open and vulnerable to receive energy, to participate in relationships and maintain a sense of wonder is not easy.

It is uncomfortable and challenging to surrender to the wisdom of being who you are in the context of a world that wants you to be the same and yet needs you to be different.

Your distinct natural being, with all the talent, wisdom and perspective you have, is the very reason you are here—and it is that which makes your life matter in ways you may not ever know. Going beyond your conditioned logical limitations—beyond reason—is the process of going beyond the bounds of your comfort zone, beyond what others expect, and beyond what seems reasonable to truly transform into who you are meant to be in a meaningful, singular, and significant way.

The GEENI System is the solution to these challenges because when you know how to discern the bigger picture from current circumstances, opportunities, and relationships, you can gain fresh perspective. Perspective is clarity. And clarity is power in creating results.

When you have clarity, you know what your next steps are...you can see problems as invitations for growth...you can make decisions that are aligned with your deeper truth, and very likely, accelerate your results. Why? Because when you know what you know and commit to acting accordingly, obstacles will melt away and resources will appear as if by magic.

Think back to the last time you really wanted something significant that you got...not a pack of gum, but something that *really* mattered to you. Whatever it was, there were likely barriers in getting it and a concern you might not get it—until you decided to make it happen. In that moment, you may not have realized it but you put all the forces at your disposal to work to bring in that outcome. And, in retrospect, if you had to do it over again, it would be even easier the next time around because you would have clarity around what to do.

That is the point of GEENI—to give you the clarity you need in any circumstance, situation, opportunity, relationship or challenge point through fresh perspective. This is a 5-part system that will show you how to ask better questions, to expand your possibilities and discover your inner knowingness around your current focus.

By the way, if you're impatient or want to get started with a 7-day ecourse, head over to **www.GeeniForChange.com** right now.

When Do You Need GEENI?

Real transformation sneaks up on you. Maybe you have experienced that moment—that face-palm, slap to the forehead instant—when you realize you are in the middle of unplanned, unexpected, unpredicted life change. It can feel like all the air just got sucked out of the room when you figure it out because real transformation changes everything. What was can no longer be, not because you don't want it but because it just won't work in your life anymore. Who you were then is not who you are now...and the 'now' you cannot be put back into the smaller container of who you were 'then.'

Basically, when you change, everything else changes. When you see everything 'out there' changing, it's time to look within.

When the rhythm of your life changes, using GEENI can be helpful to create more intentional transformation. The new cadence to how things flow, or don't flow, in your life can start out small and get bigger over time as needed to get your attention (depending on if you ignore, deny, neglect or avoid it). Or it may seem like it's happening all at once—various aspects of your life feel like they are each crumbling or imploding at virtually the same time.

Incidentally, the more 'raw' your current circumstances feel, meaning more irritating, painful, or negative, the greater the contrast between where you are and where you want to be...it is the degree of contrast that can signal the speed of the transformation process.

We like to think we can see what's coming and adapt proactively. We pride ourselves on managing all the spinning plates and bouncing balls while making a great living and having a great social life and staying fit and ... and ... and.... The reality is that, even if we see what's coming, transformation usually arrives ahead of our schedule for it because we think we have enough time to address it as it comes 'later' (and, by definition, later never comes).

There is a bonus to feeling like it's happening all at once in that you can often create the most dramatic change in that moment. Big upheavals mean big change, and if you start creating intentionally in that moment, you can often influence the forces of change that are happening anyway to bring you more of what you want.

At any rate, chances are that if it feels like transformation is happening all at once, you can look back and trace the beginnings of where it started. It could be that the current situation is reflecting a challenge or issue that you didn't get handled the first time around for some reason.

Whatever is happening in your life right now, there are signs that indicate change is on the way—it's the nature of life to change, because not-change is, ultimately, death. So it's time to be intentional about how you are showing up through the change process so you can proactively create what you want.

One of the most pervasive signs is you feel a vague sense of restlessness, of unease, of wanting something but not knowing what it is. It's an irking feeling that I describe as feeling like a Lamborghini stuck behind a lawnmower. It can feel evasive but gnawing, like registering a sound that bugs you but not placing it until you realize it's the refrigerator humming (which we often don't even notice until it's off!). A sense of restlessness is the pre-adrenaline rush that is preparing you for fight or flight until you figure out that there is a bigger reason for why you feel the way you do. To the degree you feel restless is to the degree change is imminent for you.

You'll see that things around you are breaking, not working anymore, or even ending—like physical things in your home, including appliances, light bulbs, doorbells, or furniture. It could be projects where you just aren't on track due to circumstances seemingly beyond your control—clients who are taking their business elsewhere or making unusual requests—or it could be routines or habits you have difficulty with or just don't follow through on anymore. A big one is relationships that no longer fit you or haven't grown with your life flow.

Our relationships are our mirrors, so if we don't like what we see, it's time to pay attention to that quality in ourselves as a positive pattern-interrupt. You might go through a time where you are communicating but people aren't hearing or understanding you. Maybe they are telling you to slow down, to take a break when you know you need to keep going or even speed up. It seems they don't understand or relate to you anymore. The reality is you are no longer pacing your relationships the same way as in the past. It may come to choosing whether the relationship can be repaired or if it just needs to be replaced with someone who is more in alignment with who you are now.

Another thing that could "break" is your body. If you are having odd little accidents, or health twinges, or something different happening with your body, it is a sign that things are out of whack somehow and need positive change to get back to normal operation. Things breaking could include your car, which is what gets you places; if your car is out of commission, you are standing still.

You may find that your personal preferences change, sometimes dramatically. Maybe you used to like wearing a particular clothing style or color, and suddenly that no longer suits you. Or it could be that your favorite food used to be cake and now it's fresh vegetables.

OVERVIEW AND EXPLANATION OF THIS BOOK 19

Sometimes it's even as light as changing your computer settings or favorite tv shows, or preferred genre of books and movies.

A significant sign you are ready to create change is when you start receiving messages. You start noticing things in a different way, such as billboard signage speaking to you or the radio song singing to you. Maybe unusual sights pique your interest, like squirrels showing up to escort you as you take your morning walk. Maybe you take notice of people who you aren't naturally drawn to for some reason, and suddenly you see them in a different light. Or people are saying the same thing in different ways and at different times—you notice a thread, a message in their words.

Speaking of words, it could be that your language changes—both your inner and your outer voice changes vocabulary, tense or subject choice. Your outer world is an expression of your inner world, so when your inner world is full of fear, your outer world will likely have all kinds of potential threats. If your inner world expects great things, your outer world will likely be offering them. Opportunities are attracted to you by your thoughts.

Opportunities are all potential realities, waiting for you to choose to act on them. You don't need to generate opportunities because they will find you in magnetic attraction to your thoughts, beliefs, and being. Rather, opportunities are already yours—it's about choosing to pursue them or not.

Repetitive challenges are another signal of change. When you are looping through the familiar scenery of any situation, like a 'discussion' with a project partner or attracting the same not-right client or finding yourself with the same cash flow issues *again*, you are being gifted with the opportunity to identify the pattern and resolve it on your terms. If you do not step up to the challenge, you will experience that same situation again but it will be bigger, badder, and bolder because it needs to get your attention. Do yourself a favor and see it in the moment so you can break the cycle before it breaks you. You do not need to suffer; you only need to wake up to your own life.

All these signs are measures of the degree of change for which you are making space. It's like having a full shelf—if it's already full, you have no place to put the new things you buy. You need to make space on the shelf to accommodate your new items. So, to the degree things are breaking, not working, ending, and releasing is to the degree you can expect things to change.

Remember the richest rewards often come from the most difficult situations. Transformation looks like it happens on the outside but the reality is that it changes you from the inside. It's not what happens to you but how you handle it that determines your character and your quality of life. What will you do with the cards you have been dealt? This is the pivot point question transformation offers *if* you can step see it in—or at least after—the moment of change.

That's what GEENI empowers you to do.

Who Am I and Why Should You Listen to or Trust Me?

I've worked with thousands of clients ready for significant change to help them have the clarity needed to bust out of their status quo. Clarity is the key for stepping into their personal power to make new decisions, take focused action, and accelerate their results in having the business (and life!) they really want.

My perspectives have been shared in the media (CBS, FOX, NBC, ABC). I've spoken to audiences with hundreds of people and have been a guest on radio shows, podcasts, and telesummits. I was recognized as one of WE Magazine's top women in ecommerce, have won awards for business and been endorsed by hundreds of clients for my innovative approach to getting fresh results.

I've written more than a dozen books, have contributed to numerous magazines and blogs, and am a columnist for a new thought magazine. Back in the day, Wallace Wattles, Catherine Ponder, and James Allen were new thought authors; I'm honored to be following in their footsteps.

I think it's reasonable to say I have witnessed, facilitated, and experienced accelerated business results in a variety of scenarios that bypassed what was deemed logical. In fact, the most dramatic results and subsequent transformation were often inspired through intuitive insights. What motivates me and stirs my soul is being able to help my clients get these accelerated results and change their lives very quickly (sometimes minutes!). And that's what this book is about...

By having this system, you can gain perfect clarity in the moment, regardless of the individual details of the situation. The principles behind the system are universal in nature. All they depend on is you asking and being willing to receive and act on the clarity that surfaces in response to your question(s).

Business loves speed. The GEENI System gives you a way to take the fastest path to creating results. In some cases, my clients have literally shaved *years* off what they had planned to do by getting clarity!

What would you rather do? Keep doing the same thing over and over based on what you have been taught by others or access the profound, game-changing insights that are aligned with your truth as the shortest path to *your* success?

When you use the GEENI System to bypass your conditioned limitations and activate your intuitive potential, you will find new options and opportunities beyond anything you may have considered previously. This is not about conventional business but, instead, about using conventional tools in unconventional ways with innovative strategies based on who you are and what you know through your business.

Since I have used this system with many clients, I'll share real-life scenarios to demonstrate the teachings. (Client names and identities of real customers will be changed—but the stories are real.)

With what you are about to learn, you can practically guarantee your intuition will be sparked and your clarity will be engaged. Here's to accelerating the business results you want so you can finally arrive in your best life.

The Secret Sauce: Your Perception

Perception is everything. Meaning, how you interpret the world around you will determine the quality of your experience in both life and business.

You learned how to perceive the world as a child, when your parents and authority figures told you what to believe and were your role models for living those perceptions. Most people have never questioned their beliefs in an objective way. And yet, those beliefs, perceptions and interpretations are what create their life and business as it is today.

While you are not your business, it is a reflection of you. Therefore, there is a direct connection between who you are and the results you are getting in your business. The good news is that, when you know who you are from your own truth, the results you get can change quickly.

Many entrepreneurs do not understand what it means to finally 'arrive'—meaning to feel whole, complete, fulfilled, present, and free—in ever-evolving circumstances. The truth is that 'finally arriving' is a bit like when you have finished a long journey…you get out of the vehicle you've been traveling in, step into the place you are staying in and let out a sigh of happiness, relief, and knowingness that you are where you wanted to be after the journey. Except, when you are an entrepreneur, the journey doesn't really ever end. So how does one finally arrive when in business?

The trick of it is that the feeling of having finally arrived in business is an internal experience vs. an external destination. It's a way of being vs. being done. Surfing the continuously changing circumstances of being a business owner is best done by having clarity, confidence in yourself and your decisions, and handling the discomfort of going beyond your comfort zone on a regular basis.

With the reward being your happiness, freedom, and having the life and business you want on your own terms, what would clarity be worth to you? How often have you wished to have a predictable way to know what to do when making decisions? When was the last time you thought there was another way but didn't know how to sort out what it was? That's what GEENI can help you do.

When you know what you know, you are not open to receive something innovative—something that doesn't have a place or reference point in what you already know. You simply don't know to look for an answer that is outside your current perceptions. Almost everything you do daily comes from your history—what you know is known, expected, and familiar. In other words, your biology—your need for safety based on what you have already experienced and know is safe (whether it is what you want or not)—is your primary guidance system.

Additionally, being human means we want to believe we are right in what we know. So, of course, we look for ways to prove ourselves right. This naturally reinforces that what we already know is the right way to perceive our experience. We work from what is right (by what we know) vs. what is possible. So, again, it does not invite us to step outside what we already know by virtue of judging what is right by what is known.

THE SECRET SAUCE: YOUR PERCEPTION

The reality is your beliefs, history, and actions have gotten you to where you are now. When you want something different, you'll need to shift or expand your perceptions so you can clarify your beliefs, see your options, and choose new actions to get fresh results. What got you 'here' will not get you 'there.'

It's also hard to know what 'there' is all about because you haven't experienced it yet. You have no frame of reference for what that will be like... your only toolbox is what you already know and it's not enough to craft a new experience. Resolution of old situations, circumstances, and relationships comes through replay vs. actively working toward gaining new perceptions.

In fact, many times you might feel like you are looping through old, familiar patterns like attracting the same clients with the same challenges, marketing the way you always have, finding yourself with the same results even though you were aiming for something different. I call that 'hitting your 3:00' because it's like clockwork—3:00 will always come around again. The difference is you can grow and have different tools and resources to handle your next 3:00 growth opportunity (challenge) when it comes around again. So, while your 3:00 is familiar, you can change and be ready to handle it in a different way every time it comes around which, in turn, changes your experience.

However, handling your 3:00 in a new way means you need to uplevel your perceptions and grow your capacity. You need to know what you want (vs. living in vague fantasy). You need to bypass the limitations of your logical mind which are intrinsically designed to keep you safe when reaching for new possibilities. In my experience, that kind of clarity comes from activating your intuitive potential.

There is one other factor which can influence your experience to create unexpected outcomes. That is, you may not be quite ready for the clarity—and, therefore, the changes—you think you want. That's

> **Bonus Tool**
>
> Visit **www.LynnScheurell.com/ready** to get a free self-assessment to see how ready you really are for creating the changes you want in life and business.

not a bad thing! It simply means you know the magnitude of what will change by having more clarity and you need some preparation time.

When I work with clients personally, I practice deep listening to discover the cues of my client's intuitive answers which they might not be getting on their own, and then reflect my perceptions. However, by having the GEENI System, my clients can get some level of insight on their own in the moment. So often the need to make decisions in business is NOW; my intention is that they—and now you—have a tool to get new clarity in the moment.

As Socrates supposedly said, *"What screws us up the most in life is the picture in our head of what it's supposed to be."*

Let's get into the GEENI System to help you finally arrive—beyond your logical limitations—to the clarity of your truth.

The GEENI System Explained

When was the last time you felt happy with all aspects of your life? When you felt comfortable in your own skin? That you reveled in the full knowingness that everything in your world is positively just the best and just for you?

If it's been awhile, or, if you can't even imagine any of the above, you're not alone. Most people don't even take pause to think such

THE SECRET SAUCE: YOUR PERCEPTION

things are possible so, by virtue of reading this book, you are a pioneer in creating positive life change for yourself.

Positive change is the crux of GEENI. Let's set the stage for using the GEENI System successfully.

First, it's virtually impossible to tie a financial outcome or hard deliverable to the insights and milestones of your personal intuition. And yet, many entrepreneurs make the mistake of focusing only on tactics, strategies, and techniques without considering their own wisdom.

The truth—and the paradox—of business success is this:

> *Your business can only grow as fast as you do.*

Your business success has relatively little to do with mechanics in comparison to your presence and clarity in making decisions and taking action. It's less about the decisions you make but *why* you make them and who you are choosing to become in the process.

Business isn't about what you do as much as it is about how you line up with it. It is about your congruence of thought, word, and behavior. It's about the synergy between who you are and how your business is expressing that, as well as what your customers expect and how you deliver on that promise.

Alignment requires clarity. The transformation that is required to be successful through clear alignment in business can be rigorous. The good news is the GEENI System can make it easier and save years of time, energy, sweat, and tears (of frustration and/or disappointment) when you learn what you can't see on your own right now.

> *"You cannot find your soul with your mind, you must use your heart. You must know what you are feeling. If you don't know what you are feeling, you will create unconsciously. If you are unconscious of an aspect of yourself; if it operates outside your field of awareness, that aspect has power over you."*
>
> ~ Gary Zukav

To break it down, there is a magic 'recipe' for success through entrepreneuring:

1. **Inspiration**—fueled by your calling to help people through what you do.
2. **Intelligence**—expressed through strategy, systems, and marketing.
3. **Integration**—of who you are with what you're doing in your business.

With the GEENI System, you can 'fill up' on all three aspects of that recipe by accessing clarity from a fresh perspective. Some of the benefits you can experience from clarity include:

- **Discernment:** seeing the best options amongst many.
- **Connection:** between your inner landscape and outer expression.
- **Decompression:** of emotional tension to see, create and attract new options.
- **Literacy:** understanding the language and insights from your intuition.
- **Power:** accessing new levels of personal power and self-sovereignty (of being your own supreme ruler).
- **Perspective:** seeing (and inviting) the growth potential in challenges.
- **Confidence:** gained by deep understanding and navigating circumstances easier.

And there are others, naturally. The point is all these benefits come through clarity, which is the outcome of using the GEENI System.

'GEENI' is an acronym for a powerful system of understanding life. Think of it as having your own personal genie to bring you anything you want—except the truth is you are your own genie.

Defining GEENI

As a result of working with and studying people, along with their individual situations and circumstances, for two decades, a pattern for determining where to start creating change has emerged. When people stumble onto it, it feels like magic, because things seem to open in a nearly effortless way. They get the lessons or understanding clearly and easily and can apply it to get to their next level—almost like graduation from one grade to the next.

This pattern is both unique and universal at the same time. By looking at one's own life using a universal "filter," it is possible to understand a much larger context with all the potent possibilities within it.

That is, drawing on universal principles to have the largest perspective possible for viewing an individual life in the moment gives a unique snapshot of what is right now along with the mystery of what could be from that point forward. It is unique to the individual but is universal in both possibility and consequence in relation to others (who are all, incidentally, individuals having their own experience!).

This is the core of the GEENI System. It is looking at one's own life through the objective "lens" of universal laws and principles, to understand where there is a disconnect from what is and what you want. The goal is to close the gap between where you are and where you want to be by creating intentional change through focused action.

The other thing to remember as you work through the GEENI for Change process is what Einstein said—"*the same mind that created the problem cannot solve it.*" While the seeds of the solution are in the problem, it is still necessary to add outside perspective to gain clarity. That is, it's necessary to stop the normal brain "chatter" to get new ideas.

Just because you haven't been able to do that on your own doesn't mean you are wrong—it means you are human and just haven't learned what you need to yet!

Following is a quick summary of the GEENI System.

G = Greater Truth

E = Energy

E = Environment

N = Natural Intelligence

I = Integrity

Sounds simple, right? However, when you really look at what's happening in each of these areas, you can discover some complex and amazing insights about yourself.

Throughout the rest of the book, we'll take each component and explore it fully. The main thing to remember is each area of your life contains cues and clues about what is happening for you, and each has an impact on the others.

A Word About Change

One more foundational concept must be established before we move forward in helping you create fresh results, which, by definition, means change. It is the following.

Change is the only constant. Change is everywhere. And change is the definition of life itself because life force energy naturally creates new life (results).

And yet, it's the one thing we humans naturally resist. We don't like change, especially if we didn't create it (and sometimes even if we did!).

THE SECRET SAUCE: YOUR PERCEPTION

Biologically, our brains are wired against change as a protection against anything unfamiliar, unknown or unexpected. In a state of change, we go past the status quo which triggers all our primitive warning systems and conditioned limitations to go off as a warning against the change—even if it is what we want.

The good news is you can bypass those warnings by seeing what you already know with fresh perspective. Once you understand what is happening as an opportunity and how you are responsible for creating it, you can be at choice about what you create next. Change becomes your new best friend and you can flow with the natural rhythms of life (instead of resisting what *is* . . .). ;+)

A key to success is your ability to recognize you are already changing—in every moment. You are not who you were six months ago, six weeks ago, yesterday, or even six minutes ago.

To paraphrase an unknown but wise philosopher, "it's impossible to step in the same river twice." It is impossible for you to go back to who you were 'before' and you must be who you are now with the belief you have the power to create who you are going to be next.

As you shift into heightened perception, your world will shift as well. Why?

Because your world (your results, relationships and circumstances) is your external body—it is simply a reflection of who you are on the inside. And inside, you are a dynamic interplay of thoughts, feelings, emotions, decisions, and actions—all of which is expressing through you every day. What you see 'out there' is simply an echo of 'in here.'

As you see your current results with clarity, you access new levels of personal power and new options to create different results. In other words, the GEENI System is a shortcut to getting what you want faster and easier.

How to Use GEENI

Throughout my life, I have had to struggle to make things fit for me. It often seemed I was on the outside, looking in to what everybody else was doing because whatever it was "fit" them (clothes, social activities, seminars, etc.), but it didn't fit me. I longed for flexibility in applying whatever I needed (learned, discovered, experienced, knew, etc.) from whatever system I was trying to model (participate in, learn from, be "cool" with, etc.). People thought I was a maverick rebel, just trying to make things harder for them as a result, although I was really trying to absorb and assimilate so it made sense for me.

As a result, the GEENI System is designed for maximum flexibility. It is a "one size fits all" without being specific, but still giving structure so you can take it and make it work for the best possible outcome for you. It is designed with the end in mind, which is clarity about your being and your life so you can create success by your own definition. That is, after all, what you, and only you, are accountable for—your result(s) in the end.

One of the most beneficial, flexible aspects of the GEENI System is that you can start wherever it makes the most sense for you. You can start with the area that resonates for you right now or use reverse psychology and work your way in from what least resonates. You can go in order of the acronym, GEENI, or pick one and work that for a while until you're ready to tackle another one.

However, the idea is that each aspect plays off the others. It is ideal to consider the effects of each relative to the other so you can create a more decisive, comprehensive, bolder intention and corresponding action plan. Each area weaves in and out and through the other, but they stand on their own as well.

It is also your choice as to how deep you want to delve into each area. You may decide to go with whatever comes up at first glance or go all the way to the bottom to explore how each area has shown up throughout your life. The value in considering it from a longer time vantage point is you can look for the source of your pattern over time. You aren't merely looking at current results, or symptoms, but at root cause of your world. You can look sequentially, at that one issue/pattern at a time, or chronologically at what patterns have presented in a given timeframe to discover their current state of resolution.

The GEENI System can also be applied to virtually any life situation, be it relationship, finances, health, home, social life, reputation, career, etc. Once you consider each of these five areas for any given life situation, you may see that it is isolated to that life area, but more likely, you will see how it spills over into other areas. There is a great quote by someone wise and anonymous that says *"how you do anything is how you do everything."* The GEENI System will show you what you need to know in one thing, or everything to create positive change—it is completely up to you.

Asking Quality Questions for Clarity

As you are likely starting to see by now, the GEENI System is a proven process for transformational change that can be applied to anything in life or business, in relationships or circumstances, to situations and challenges. It can also upgrade what is going well to having that go even better.

Of course, the degree of result is up to you. Your changes and results will reflect your ability to be honest and clear on who you are, what you're doing and how you're showing up in the world. That naturally infers that you need to be willing to ask the questions and then receive the insights that surface through the answers.

So how do you ask good questions and know you are getting the insights you need? You'll know you have what you need when you feel your system relax (body and mind). You might feel lighter, happier or calmer. You might feel a surge of energy as the 'old' releases.

You might feel inspired to act on your clarity right away. Whatever it looks like for you, it's having the courage to ask the questions that will get you there.

Exploring your unseen insights through questions gives your wisdom a channel, a conduit, to express. You might find simple yes/no questions asked in a progressive way work best. As an example, see the following:

- Is making this decision necessary right now? Yes.
- Do I have what I need to make this decision right now? No.
- Is there something else I need to know to make this decision right now? Yes.
- Can I learn this information immediately? Yes.
- Is this information about someone I know? Yes.
- Is this information related to a client? Yes.
- Is this information about my fear that they won't get results? No.
- Is this information about my ability to receive in return from my client? Yes.
- Will this information affect our timing in working together? Yes.
- Is it the best and highest use of my time to work with this client right now? No.

Essentially, you keep asking questions as you follow the energy until you get clarity. Ask why, or what's under that, when you get an answer to keep diving into (or under) the challenges and insights.

Another question technique is to have a conversation with your intuition. Get curious and have a conversation like you would with another person. Some people like to sit with their eyes closed in silence while others like to do this while walking in nature. Your answers might not come in words but in feelings in your body.

THE SECRET SAUCE: YOUR PERCEPTION

For example, you might ask about whether you should work with a client or not right now, and the answer might be a sense of heaviness in your stomach or a slight pain somewhere in your body. You might ask why that sensation showed up—was it about them or about you? Feel which option is lighter and which is heavier, then explore either way. Pay attention to your sensations, emotions and, to a lesser degree, your thoughts (because your thoughts may be conditioned responses).

As a real-world example, one of my clients was quite distraught about her family not accepting her moving out of state. Despite being in her fifties, she wanted their approval and blessing. In using the GEENI System, she came to realize that the family dynamic was for them to withhold their emotional support so she would chase it and, therefore, stay connected with them. Essentially, it was a power struggle she unknowingly participated in for decades.

In exploring that further, she learned she would often assume personality characteristics to win people over vs. being who she was (an old coping strategy to get approval) and then felt bad about herself because she could get quite assertive (because she knew how to chase what she wanted). She worried people would find her aggressive, yet that intensity was part of what fueled her tenacity in business.

By seeing her intensity was related to her family dynamic, she was able to disconnect the two emotional responses (judgments), which clarified her ability to access her personal power without negativity, shift the dynamic with her family, make the move and be fully present with her new business opportunities.

This example shows two things. One is that challenges are usually connected to a larger internal landscape, like a giant hairball. Trying to solve a problem may touch on many predicaments and paradoxes while following a central thread so it's important to be open to what surfaces in the exploration of clarity.

Two, it is important to not judge what comes up by asking questions. Your goal is to get clarity through new insight vs. continuing as-is based on what you think you know. Nothing is good or bad—only your thinking makes it one or the other and judging what you learn only slows the process. The point is to use your intuition to bypass your conditioned limitations and gain new clarity so you can make different decisions that can result in fresh results.

After using the GEENI System for years, I can zero in on just about any business or personal challenge—even if it's a long-standing issue—and get to the insight needed for clarity in minutes. It takes practice, paying attention, asking great questions, and listening for the answers, especially if they are unexpected, unfamiliar or seemingly contradictory to the current circumstances.

The one thing that can derail your ability to use the GEENI System effectively is this—thinking "well, I'm not an intuitive person...my challenge is different...blah, blah." That is just not true. Every single person ever born has intuition. The question is whether they are accessing it or not.

Your challenges are your invitations for growth—while personal to you in this moment, it's likely you have gone through something similar in the past and now have conditioned responses to it as a result. Unless you gain fresh perspective, you will continue to do what you have always done—and that just won't do if you want to reach a new level of success.

At any rate, intuition is like a muscle—the more you use it, the stronger it is and the more distinct the messages. You were born with intuition. Your invitation now is to activate it for new clarity.

If you're confused, that's normal—just keep reading. This will become easier to understand as we move through the elements of the GEENI System.

G Stands for Greater Truth

Now that you know change is inevitable and that your world reflects your inner clarity, it's time to go beyond where you are now through the bigger picture. It's what I call the Greater Truth—the "G" in the GEENI System.

The bottom line is that everything is connected—everything. To know this for yourself, take a moment and look around your world right now. The chair you're sitting in might be part of a set, it is comprised of various material components that come from different sources, it was made by someone somewhere in the world based on a design that someone else created, and each of them have families who support an economy . . . you get the idea—and that's just one chair! When we really stop for the first time to consider how interwoven our world is with the rest of a much bigger world, it is mind-boggling.

Similarly, whatever you are experiencing in your life reflects that same concept. Much like the proverbial tip of the iceberg, life's greatest opportunities lie in what is not visible to us. In fact, it is often because it is not visible to us that you know it is your next growth opportunity, or next lesson in your life curriculum. Everything happens for, not to, you.

Others around you may not understand what you're putzing around with because they don't need that lesson, which is all the more frustrating for those of us in the middle of a lesson, or growth period. When others don't understand why we're stuck on something seemingly so evident, it is a sign we are really in the middle of big personal growth.

In the throes of intense personal development, it is important to understand there is a Greater Truth behind whatever it is that seems to be causing you difficulties. Sometimes the Greater Truth can be discovered quickly when you simply stop to consider what that could be; other times, it is more elusive and a longer discovery process. Greater Truths are based on universal principles but are unique in how they manifest in each person's life. Remember your Greater Truths are for you, not for anyone else, and vice-versa.

Following are some different ways to consider the Greater Truth of your current situation.

A Greater Truth will show up time and time again, especially when it is not recognized. Consider it a thread that runs through several different types of situations or experiences, or maybe even through your whole life. It is something that shows up again and again and again, creating a predictability of sorts as a pattern over time.

Take the story of Marie* (client name changed) who, at age 50, found herself unhappy yet again after seemingly changing her whole life. She had been unhappy with her life, living in a small apartment for many years, in a stagnant relationship, in a going nowhere job where she felt unappreciated for her true talents and not making enough money. She decided to geographically move her life and rent a home that was somewhat out of her budget but affordable if she cut back on extras. She started a new job and took a break from the ten-year relationship that didn't offer any future.

Within six months, she discovered she mostly liked her new home, but wasn't sure about the new locale. She went back to the dysfunctional relationship (with distance now being a factor) and didn't like her new job as she felt not only underappreciated by her colleagues but under attack for her femininity and, adding insult to injury, wasn't making enough money. (Incidentally, upon doing her taxes the first year after her move, she realized that she made $92,000 that year but was unaware of it and had nothing to show for it.) It seemed she was in pretty much the same place even after changing apparently everything and she needed help to see what happened.

Upon working with the GEENI System, she admitted her family had deemed her a "pretty baby doll." In her youth, she had used her beauty to earn money as an exotic dancer and had turned to alcohol and drugs to numb herself from the attention of unsavory men. She never expected to be able to earn a living through her skills and talents because she was "pretty" and "not smart enough," but had gone to college because she needed to prove something to herself. Can you see the threads in her life? She couldn't.

The Greater Truths for Marie were around...

- deserving the money that she earned from her intelligence and talents,
- having a significant relationship that honored all of her being (not just physical),
- living and working in supportive and healthy environments,
- cultivating her own innate talent and skills,
- loving her beauty from the inside out,
- honoring, accounting for and being in gratitude for the money she did earn, and,
- accepting all of who she is now versus who others said or thought she was without seeking external validation from anybody else.

These are significant Greater Truths that took fifty years to emerge and be recognized. Do you see yourself in any of them?

Could Marie have done it faster? Maybe. However, if she could have done it faster to avoid the pain, she would not have experienced the depth of her lessons. In growth, there is always some pain involved, because what 'was' must, essentially, die to allow the birthing energy of new life experiences to begin. Had Marie not experienced the range of what she did, her life would be a different story and her lessons would have shown up differently.

For example, consider your own life as a giant tapestry. From the front, you can see the beautiful colors and intricate patterns that are unique to you. From the back, you see all the unfinished threads, the unsightly knots, the places it wants to unravel. If you pulled on any one of those threads to try to make the back more visually pleasing, you would unravel what makes the front so beautiful. It is because of the individual threads that the pattern is beautiful. If you don't like the pattern, or Greater Truth, you are seeing in your own life, you can change it but you must see it first.

Your experiences, or Greater Truths, show up over time and will create patterns to help you make sense of your world. These patterns create a frame of reference to create order to what you experience. Understanding your reference points will point the way to your Greater Truths.

For example, to continue with Marie's story, her reference point was that her physical beauty was the only thing of value about her. While she is indeed a beautiful woman, we know this is simply not true because her outer beauty only scratches the surface of her true beauty.

However, this reference point created a whole pattern for her in not being recognized for her contributions at work because she was too pretty, in not being paid enough because she felt put off to the side as others got raises, in never feeling "smart enough" to be a real player in management.

This was also her reference point for creating relationships that couldn't give her true sustenance, in how she related to women professionally and personally, and in using various substances to numb her intuitive sensitivities from unscrupulous men attracted to her superficially but from who she received validation for what her family seemed to prize most about her... and all from one reference point.

The big question for you is: what's your reference point?

Results also demonstrate our Greater Truths. That is, where we are now is a result of the decisions and choices we made in our past. Those decisions and choices were the best we could make at the time, given our resources and awareness then. Our current results give us a key as to where our Greater Truths can make the biggest difference.

If we look at Marie's current results, we see that she moved to a new locale but held on to an old relationship despite the dysfunction and lack of future. All she changed was the venue. She felt unfulfilled, with a vague sense of something better but clinging to the crumbs of what good she gleaned from analyzing and reframing what was in the relationship. She paid homage to the history, and desperately tried to see the positive in this man who was contributing only a minimal amount of time and effort to their relationship. Her analysis showed she wasn't getting what she wanted in a relationship. Her Greater Truth was that she didn't believe she deserved it because she was "only" a pretty face.

Another factor in being aware of Greater Truths at work in our lives is the significance of what we are doing, the significance of the impact of the Greater Truth. Are you making a difference? Is being aware of the Greater Truth going to make a significant difference in how you create your world?

For Marie, she was working in higher-level corporate positions, and changed jobs three times in four years. The significance of her contribution was undervalued but she didn't realize it was because she undervalued it. She was doing her work because of being expected to do it as a job rather than doing her work out of the passion and true talent that was the motivator for her to get into her field of work. It was a case of performance versus true contribution.

When she did change jobs, she consistently created more of what she wanted but didn't recognize her success in doing so. She continued to find reasons to be disillusioned because she couldn't see the significance of her true gifts and contribution. When presented with ideas on how to be a voice for her passion as an industry avant-garde leader, she couldn't comprehend how that could be possible, much less her true purpose. She couldn't see her own significance.

Like Marie, if we don't see our Greater Truths, they will continue to show up again and again until we see our pattern. Our collective purpose here is to learn, to work with our threads, and to understand consciously what we are creating. If we ignore, deny, neglect or avoid this responsibility, it will present itself another time, another way, and usually in a bigger, louder way to get our attention. In other words, it is up to you to get through all the noise and distractions to get to your Greater Truth so you can move to your next level.

There can be moments where it feels like you have Greater Truths that conflict, such as your awareness that you are a valuable being and your awareness that you need to earn a living despite feeling undervalued in the moment. However, with reflection, you can see the Greater Truth at work is the one that says you are valuable because it is the one that will bring you to your best and greatest good in the long run.

A Greater Truth is positive, personal, and is based on universal principles. A Greater Truth also withstands the test of time, is simple, and just feels right.

You may be aware of Greater Truths in the lives of people around you. If that is the case, you can see them because you have a matching picture with them on that truth. Now you may have already handled it, but it could also be a mirror for you to see that truth in your own life more clearly.

For example, if you notice people are consistently late in meeting or calling you as previously agreed, look at the value of time in your own life. Are you valuing time the way you have agreed to with yourself and others?

Once you understand the Greater Truths at work in your life, having passed through the growth period that helped you learn them, you are free to apply what you've learned and move on. However, there may, and hopefully will, be new Greater Truths you have the opportunity to understand. When you get to a point where you understand all your Greater Truths, you no longer need to be on this physical plane.

If you look back through your life at your Greater Truth discovery process, you can see that what used to confound you is now just a part of who you know yourself to be; that is, if a situation were to occur for a Greater Truth that you already know about, it is no longer the challenge it was at one time. There are some who would say that this alone is what determines "enlightenment"—the ability to handle what would have thrown you off at a previous time in your life. Once you know how to handle that Greater Truth situation, it is no longer necessary for it to present in your life... *you got it.*

Get Started with G Now

Look around your business world right now—your work, clients, colleagues and peers, office environment, cash flow...yes, everything. How does it look? More specifically, how do you feel when you look at the various elements that comprise your business life? Wherever you see an indicator you aren't happy, there could be a Greater Truth at work.

Remember, a Greater Truth is a thread that runs through various situations but ties them all together in a continuous kind of way.

> Do you attract the same kind of less-than-ideal clients over and over again?
>
> Do you get into the same kinds of undesirable or boring projects repeatedly, with different gigs or clients, that share a pattern?
>
> Do you feel like you are in familiar but uncomfortable situations—a lot?
>
> Do you reach a certain level of success but can't quite seem to grow beyond that point?

One client couldn't figure out why she always had a lot of drama—until she realized she was creating new results through destruction. It was like she would blow up the house to redecorate the room. Once she understood her Greater Truth in how she created could be less destructive, she could actively choose how she brings in new results—cleaner, easier, and smoother.

Another client didn't know why he wasn't attaining celebrity status—until he learned he didn't have the energy required to create that outcome. The Greater Truth of being a celebrity is the 'always on' factor. Despite his head defining success as being a celebrity, everything else about him wanted a more relaxed lifestyle. Now he is enjoying where he is in the moment with his career (and, ironically, the press is starting to seek him out).

One of the most challenging aspects of being an entrepreneur is creating "the constants." Business, by nature, is dynamic. Being solid in an ever-evolving landscape requires constant shifting while standing strong in what we know, being open while having boundaries, doing what we do without always knowing the outcomes. We need to follow our own truth even when it seems to defy rationality.

Entrepreneuring is about finding the courage to embrace dreams in the face of intimidating circumstances, including perceived lack of time, resources, relationships, and all the various priorities and new project ideas that keep coming non-stop.

We have to keep business going even as we are in personal transformation. It's like trying to change a tire while driving your car at freeway speed, on a road you've never been on before, in a car that feels like it needs some service. Who does that... every day??? You and every other entrepreneur out there. It's part of what pulls us forward every day.

Sometimes we entrepreneurs are swimming against the tide of social thought (these are dark times, the economy is terrible, blah, blah, blah) and our friends and family think we're crazy. It can be difficult to keep your vision, much less act on making it happen.

That's exactly why you need to create your own "constants"... those things that help anchor your experience and support you in your personal clarity. Now—more than ever—it is really, really important for you to invest in yourself and your business, have hope about the future and gain even more clarity in everything you do. These are the best of times and possibly the darkest of times...it's all in how you perceive what's happening in your world.

As an entrepreneur, you're used to seeing opportunities where others don't—and, throughout history, may people have positioned themselves in the 'dark' times for unbelievable success because they acted exactly when it seemed most counter-intuitive to logical or superficial review. Right now, a lot of people are very successful—and will be even more so when the global economy is strong—because they followed through and acted on what they believed was right despite circumstances and even the opinions of others.

To do the same thing—be successful in your own way—you need access to what you don't already know. And you need to leverage every bit of your time... it's the only thing you can't ever get back. You MUST invest your time wisely. So, feel into your business world to discern where there is contrast between what you want and what it is now. Do you have a Greater Truth emerging?

If you feel uncomfortable somewhere in your business, it is a message. Your body never lies—feel within your body your response to specific areas of your business so your mind can give it words. Once you have the words, write them down so you can see and consider them.

For example, if you think of waking up tomorrow morning to work with a particular client, and you notice your chest feels tight or your palms get sweaty or you imagine just going back to sleep, that's a sign. Using your questioning technique from the previous chapter, ask if there is a Greater Truth to this client, the focus of your work together or something else... keep asking different, related questions until you get new clarity.

If you aren't sure what you are feeling, that's good because you are open to your Greater Truth(s). The not-knowing feeling is the only place where you both seek and are willing to learn something beyond your conditioned responses. Simply sit with yourself for a few minutes, let your mind get quiet and see what messages come forward.

A Personal G Story

Here is a personal story about when I discovered a Greater Truth for myself. It's from when I was just starting out as a Feng Shui consultant. (Feng Shui remains one of my true loves to this day . . . but I digress!) ;+)

Anyway, at the time, I was charging $75 per consultation. I had no time limits on how long a session lasted—the longest one was 11 hours (truth!). And I couldn't GIVE a session away!

I hired a business coach who told me I needed a higher fee. I thought she was out of her mind—raise my fees when I wasn't attracting business as it was??? Holy cow . . . but, her parting words as she went on vacation for three weeks was to meditate on a new number as my rate going forward.

Me being me, I meditated on a number that same night and got one. Since she was going to be gone for a while and I couldn't check in with her, I decided to put that number into action immediately. (Once you get to know me better, you'll find out that things happen fast in my world!)

The first time I said that new number out loud to a potential client, I'm not sure how he heard it over the sound of my knocking knees. But I held my breath, acted like it was the most natural thing in the world and, over the course of the next three weeks, I had more consultations than I'd had in the previous three months at the lower rate!

When my business coach returned from vacation, we had a session. Of course, she asked if I had a new number and I said yes and that I'd been using it already. She asked what my new rate was—and remember, she knew my fee was $75. When I told her $450—and that I was GETTING it! I'm pretty sure she fell off her chair.

The point is that, once I was charging enough, people believed I was offering something of value. I was more in line with the market in terms of fees. I didn't need to 'wait' for some reason to justify my new fees based on filling my schedule at the lower rate first. And I was getting booked right and left at my new rate.

It felt great to receive my value professionally. The greater truth was I needed to honor myself and claim my worth to make it happen. Once I did, my business took off. But I had to let go of what I thought I knew, follow the answer I got, put it into action and be ready for new results.

To make this story relevant to you, here is how you know if you are pricing your offers properly—you feel good about your work with clients.

If you feel drained, resentful, anxious, frustrated, watch the clock during your time together, stressed about money, feel like you can't breathe, feel rushed, pushed or hurried in your session time or conversations, then a boundary around your worth is being violated through your pricing.

You are the only one who can set and honor your boundaries. You are the only person who can set your fees. From what I have seen, most entrepreneurs undervalue their work by at least 10%—and that likely includes you.

You may not have a pricing strategy in place, or have one that doesn't serve you, or have pricing that doesn't convey your worth. You need to know your value—based on the degree of positive transformation your clients experience as well as how you feel in delivering on your brand promise—and claim it through your fees. It's how the Universe rewards you for applying your gift to help others.

Your rates must make sense within a strategic framework or business model. If you don't have a business model, you're flying blind and it's likely your business feels scattered. If you can't predict your monthly income in advance, it's time for an overhaul in your rates, your relationship with your business, and your business model.

The Sacred Exchange

There is another Greater Truth that we need to talk about here, especially because it relates to the above. It's what I call the 'Sacred Exchange' of business.

Business happens through the transaction that occurs when a customer buys what you are selling and you deliver it. However, there is simultaneously also a Sacred Exchange occurring in that transaction in that your customer is investing in themselves through your offer. At the same time, you are being rewarded financially for packaging your ability to create transformation through that customer.

Your customer isn't simply buying what you are selling—they are investing in achieving a new outcome for themselves. You aren't just getting paid for what you did but are being rewarded for your initiative in packaging who you are as a solution.

So, just as your customer is investing in themselves through you, you are being rewarded from the Universe (higher power, collective consciousness, whatever you call it) through that customer.

For me, the Sacred Exchange is a Greater Truth of business. And it is what keeps me going, even when business seems hard—because business is a way to connect to the sacred.

What Greater Truth is present in your world? Your Greater Truth may reveal itself not only in how to fix or upgrade situations but in how you approach your work. Just like one of my Greater Truths is that there is a Sacred Exchange in business, you may have a Greater Truth that serves as a compass for your business decisions.

It's usually easier to see Greater Truths retroactively. Think back to a time when you felt great about something that happened in your business…maybe you solved a significant problem or your customer had a stellar experience with you. What was the Greater Truth of that situation, relationship, or outcome? Compare that answer with other situations in the past…when you see enough of the same patterns, a Greater Truth is confirmed.

In this case, the Greater Truth could be the uniqueness of your solution, the type of clients who benefit most by your work, the combination of factors that preclude maximum success for your clients or how you showed up in delivering on your promise.

If you are currently being challenged, stop to consider what Greater Truth is trying to surface or actualize through that challenge. Are you thinking too small? Are you working in a deal that is not quite right for you? Are you chasing the money vs. being happy? Are you working a job vs. setting up systems to deliver predictable results for your clients? Are you making your self-care a non-priority because you are so focused on business? Are you unhappy with how you are living your life because your business is not reflecting your knowingness in some way?

In summarizing the G part of the GEENI for Change process, sit and reflect on what your Greater Truths are trying to show you right now. This requires just a few minutes of your time, and it may be helpful to journal or doodle or diagram what comes up in your self-dialogue.

- What is your thread in this current situation? How does it look in a pattern?
- Is there a thread you want to unravel? Is there a pattern you want to change?
- What is your frame of reference for this situation? Is it valid for this situation?
- How can you view your current situation differently?
- As you look around your life, what are your current results?
- What results did you get that you wanted?
- What results occurred that you didn't want?
- What results haven't you noticed before?
- How can you make changes for new results?
- What is the significance of your situation right now?
- How large is the Greater Truth lesson you are experiencing?
- What can you do to see through the "noise" more clearly to get through your growth period?
- What systems are needed to help you understand and live your Greater Truths once you discover them?

Simply paying attention to the Greater Truths in your business can be a game-changer. That being said, let's move on to the first *E* in GEENI next.

E Is for Energy

Energy—this is the first "E" in the GEENI System. It's important to know the level of your positive Energy as well as where your Energy drains are—the places where you are losing life force Energy.

Even more, your Energy is always evolving you. By definition, Energy needs to flow to be in its natural dynamic state. I'm not a scientist, but I know that the movement of Energy is what generates some level of power, even at the smallest increment of its presence. The movement of Energy is what makes things go. And it is the dynamic force within your own life that makes things happen, which cumulatively becomes your evolution.

As a creature of nature, you are consistently transforming to your next level of being. However, that can take shape in different ways, based on how fast or slow your Energy is moving and how willing you are to go where it takes you.

If you resist, stop or block the Energy flow of your life, you create stagnant pools of stuck Energy that become bigger, heavier and/or denser over time. Eventually, those stuck Energy places manifest as dysfunctional relationships, unhappy business doings or an unhealthy physical body. And these are the clues to how you can support your own evolution…your stuck places are homing beacons to guide you to what needs your energetic attention.

The truly ironic part is we can always see somebody else's stuck parts more clearly than our own. There is a reason for this ... if you knew the lesson contained in your stuck places which are designed to teach you what you need, they (you) wouldn't be stuck, right? You can't see your own blind spots, because that's the source of your lesson in working with your own Energy!

However, we can see what the people around us aren't addressing for two reasons: first, we're not attached to the outcome and second, it's not our lesson to learn (or, if it is, we have a jumpstart on it because we can see it!).

Here are three things you can do right now to start working with your Energy.

1. Pay attention to the messages.

Your Energy is always "talking" to you...if you aren't experiencing the results you want in your life, your evolution is continuing in some area. If your Energy is stuck, there's a message there. If you feel a sting, ping, charge, or a desire to avoid a person, situation, or opportunity, you are being invited to consider what you need to handle for your next level. AND, by the way, when you decide to go to your next level, anything that stands in the way of you achieving that level will come up for your consideration to be handled. Just making the commitment to move toward your own best evolution will bring up messages—that's the energetic gift of your spirit.

2. Believe in your own evolution.

Know that your spirit is trying to bring you magic when it brings those "hurt-y" places to your attention. Understand you are dynamic and growing and your Energy is supporting you in going to new places in your life. Know there is a better future waiting for you, and it is your responsibility to live it as a physical expression of divine consciousness. After all, that's your reason for being—to give form to divinity and feed your experience into the greater whole! Your evolution is a microcosm of the vital growth that fuels divine consciousness in every moment. It's a big deal. ;+)

3. Get out of your own way.

Now that you know your Energy is working to help you evolve to your next best level, it's time to get out of your own way and receive your best life experience. You are inherently worthy of the most amazing life, and it's trying to come to you. By handling your stuck places proactively and consciously, as well as opening to receive all the infinite grace that has your name on it, you are no longer standing in your shadow wondering why it's dark. Sometimes this action alone can bring what you want in your life and business.

Now is an ideal time to look at where your Energy is trying to evolve you, and where you are effectively blocking your own dynamic being from your best possible expression. If you discover there is something you're not enjoying, or a nudge to try something new (much less anything you've been ignoring or neglecting), it is your Energy talking to you. Pay attention and let the Energy flow... and it's likely your life and business results will too.

Money Energy and the 7 Business Systems

As 'out there' as it may seem, money is an Energy. We humans have made that mean something. In fact, in today's world, money is a form of survival, or life force, Energy. Without money, it is hard to live in today's economically-based society.

All Energy follows the path of least resistance (think water). Money also follows the path of least resistance. Systems give Energy a path in business and are a key to making more money.

When you know what systems to put in place in your business to leverage time and resources, you automate your business' ability to generate more revenues, take advantage of new opportunities and gain momentum in the marketplace.

There are seven key systems your business MUST have in place, regardless of your industry, to maximize your revenues. While this is not a book about business systems, knowing these systems can help you use GEENI to be more effective in pinpointing where you need to focus your Energy.

1. **The Convergence Point:** Your Passion/Target Market/Offer
   You need to know why you do what you do as well as who is looking for and will most benefit by it, as well as having a strong offer.

2. **The Signature System:** Product/Service
   What you do to solve problems or meet needs must be packaged in a signature system for delivery, regardless of whether it is through a product or a service.

3. **The Marketing:** Position/Messages/Conscious Language
   Positioning is what separates competitors in the marketplace, and includes the messages and language used to describe your unique business value. Using conscious language vs. the language of information is emotionally compelling for today's savvy customers.

4. **The Pricing:** Personal Energy and Mindset/Value Recognition/How to Price
   You cannot receive more than your personal sense of worth believes you deserve—your mindset around money is a big key to your pricing. It's also important to educate your potential clients on the value your offers provide as well as having a pricing model that makes sense to your customers.

5. **Client Uptimization:** Gravity Flow / Upsell Design / How to Sell *and* Close
   Once your customers discover what you can do for them, it's important to be able to 'close' the deal through value recognition. Even more, by having an intentional gravity flow through your offers, your clients will be moved to take action—and take advantage of upsells—as a natural outcome.

6. **The Automation:** Systems / Website / Back-End Technology
   In today's digital world, your customers must experience seamless nurturing, sales, and delivery on their purchases. Likewise, you need to be able to reach your customers easily and meet their expectations based on their behavior through their buying journey with you. Automated technology is the best way to make that happen.

7. **The Platform Design:** Expert Visibility / Action Plan
   You have to be seen to sell, which means you need to have credibility, authority, and trust in your market. Being perceived as an expert, or thought leader, happens by having and implementing a strategic action plan.

If any one of these systems is compromised (or weak), it could undermine your business results. You can use GEENI to identify which business system needs the most urgent attention.

For example, ask questions like the following:

> Is one of my business systems in need of focused attention to maximize my results for effort?

> Is it X system that needs focused attention right now? (Repeat this question through all the business systems. If you get more than one system, ask if one or the other is more important or if they are related in the need for attention.)

With X being the system that needs focused attention right now, is there a Greater Truth or an Energy that is trying to express? (When you get the answer, ask if it is that answer or an Environment, then that answer or Natural Intelligence... the goal is to isolate which area of the GEENI system to work with as you ask questions.)

Once you have identified the business system and the area of GEENI to work with, follow your curiosity. For example:

With my marketing system being the focus, and Integrity being the GEENI area, is it accurate to say my messaging needs an upgrade? Is it accurate to say my language could be more meaningful to my audience? That my positioning could be more distinctive?

Keep diving in and asking questions based on the answers you get by using the GEENI System. You are looking for where your Energy is out of alignment (with your essence, your truth, your clients, your marketing, etc.). The good news is you can seed your best outcomes by aligning your Energy with what really matters as well as upgrading your external Energy sources (or people/places where you draw energy from—you'll know where they are because you feel stronger, happier, lighter, clearer, etc.).

2 Simple Shifts You Can Make Now

Two simple shifts in perspective can help you get aligned with your Energy starting right now.

First, the reality is that, once you slow down your internal speed and breathe, then release what you don't need to do, be responsible for what you decide to do and "own" your business, your business will grow because the quality of your life just got better.

You don't *have* to do anything, really...this is about *you, your* gifts, *your* contribution to the world, *your* personal transformation journey, *your* business. It's all your choice. You get to decide the quality of your experience as part of entrepreneuring. Are you running a marathon for the long haul or sprinting to a finish line? It's up to you. Both work.

Either way, you have to pace yourself for restoration and rejuvenation sometime or you will get an offer you can't refuse in your health, relationships, or business outcomes.

Personally, I have learned—the hard way—to fill up as I go on at least a weekly basis, but that wasn't always the case. Several years ago, I got 'an offer I couldn't refuse' when I discovered I had severe adrenal fatigue. I lost valuable time because I couldn't take my Energy for granted anymore—I had an instant lifestyle shift overnight to reduce stress and rebuild my system.

Second, remember to create time for spontaneous special moments when they happen. That's where the 'juice' is... here is an example from a photographer in Washington Park when he captured a young father dancing with his child in a rapturous celebration of being with the live music.

Take a few minutes to check it out and prime your joy Energy to flow:

http://youtu.be/-FPilslxdrw

Once you are in the Energy of your joy, and you are 'owning' your choices and experience, your business—and your life—take on a richer texture and there is a new flow that weaves through both. You'll probably find you get more done, you'll be more attuned to life's special moments as they happen, and your Energy will feel lighter as you do.

6 Myths Blocking People from Using Energy as a Guide

The things that block most people from going for 'it'—their most extraordinary life—and, retrospectively, living with regrets include: 1) not being willing to risk certain mediocrity for the potentially amazing, 2) thinking they have time to do it later, and, 3) assuming they can do it through mental constructs vs. soul-based intuition.

These people think Energy is not real but, in fact, Energy is all that IS real! As Carl Sagan said, *'we are made of starstuff'*. Neil deGrasse Tyson said, "*There's as many atoms in a single molecule of your DNA as there are stars in the typical galaxy. We are, each of us, a little universe.*" With that in mind, how can anyone feel trapped, stuck, lost, or in overwhelm?

The most significant challenge is thinking we can get to it on our own when, in fact, humans are social beings. We heal through sharing stories. However, not every listener is qualified to offer feedback and guidance because their own 'stuff' is in the way. If they love you, they will be risk-averse for you or try to soften the edges for you... that's why it's important to work with a system to access your own wisdom (especially if you don't have an experienced guide who is a high communicator to help you).

To break out of established patterns and habits, you need relevant messages, clear insights and a way to go beyond where you've always been. What happens if you don't work with your intuition? Nothing.

And that's the point... the thoughts you think are normal because they are your own. Where you are today WILL be where you are tomorrow because you are not doing anything to get past currently known discomfort. But it doesn't have to be like that... your tomorrow (your later today even!) can be different. All it takes is the courage to step into a new commitment to yourself.

Here are the 6 top "reasons" (myths) that people have told me about why they don't invest time in reading Energy and learning about their own intuition.

1. Not having the time or money to live their best life.

When I ask my clients how they will feel when they have what they want, most of the time it's about 'feeling relaxed', 'like I can breathe', 'I don't have to listen to anybody else'... all are experiences they can have now but deny themselves. (Ironically, when they allow living their best life now in the moment, they attract those experiences faster and easier.)

The only time to live your best life is now—and it's an internal state rather than based on external factors. The truth is there is never the right or enough time to seize the day—it's just only ever now. If you're going to wait for any reason, you will die with regrets.

Side myth 1: People think it's too late or they are too old to go for what they really want. The truth is it's never too late to be who you are and have what you want.

Side myth 2: People think it takes time to create big change—it doesn't. Instead, it takes courage. Do you have the courage to show up for yourself? Once you go through the GEENI System, you will know what is holding you back or keeping you small, such as particular relationships, your current business in the way it's structured, where you live, how you think about yourself. The GEENI System helps you identify and then answer questions like this... *but*, once your proverbial bell has rung, you cannot unring it. Then it takes accessing your internal resources to handle what you have seen and go for what you want.

2. That working with intuition is a luxury or foolish.

If you want to get to the top of a mountain, what's the fastest way—to climb step by step or take a helicopter? Working with intuition bypasses the logical mind to get to the energetic level, which is a much faster way to get what you want.

One way to work with intuition is by using a professional intuitive. People might be embarrassed or think working with a professional intuitive is not reliable, proven, or dependable, or that the people who work with an intuitive are foolish.

The truth is that very successful people have recognized the power of intuition, knowing that there is an energy that we can tap into for 'inside information' to accelerate results. Queen Elizabeth I, Napoleon III, Albert Einstein, Princess Diana, Prime Minister Tony Blair, and Andrew Carnegie had a live-in intuitive. Several U.S. Presidents have openly admitted their reliance on psychic clarity, including: George Washington, Abraham Lincoln, James Garfield, President Theodore Roosevelt, Woodrow Wilson, Warren G. Harding, Calvin Coolidge, Herbert Hoover, Franklin Delano Roosevelt, Harry Truman, John F. Kennedy, Lyndon Johnson, Richard Nixon, Ronald Reagan, and Bill Clinton. Hillary Clinton, Deepak Chopra, and even Donald Trump have consulted professional intuitives.

Celebrities like George Clooney, Brad Pitt, Sarah Jessica Parker, and Cameron Diaz have consulted intuitives. Back in the day, one of my clients worked with Patrick Swayze and wanted to introduce us. Before we could make the connection, his health deteriorated so it never happened... but it's a cool 'almost happened' story.

The truth is the possibility of being judged as foolish for working with intuition as a tool to go for 'it' is really that people are scared. Risk-takers are admired and those are the people who achieve results because they break out. No conformist ever made history. We admire those who go where we cannot go on our own. I'm not saying you need to make history...but you do need to think and create on your own so you can do what is best for you, your business, and your loved ones.

Friedrich Nietzsche said, "... *those who were seen dancing were thought to be insane by those who could not hear the music.*" The time is now to hear your music and follow it to live the life you want—nobody else is living your life. Only you can make the decision, based on your Energy and intuition, as to whether you are living the life you want—or not.

Side myth: People often believe they have to work hard for results so working with intuition is like cheating the system. But if you could compress time and get a "month's" (time is relative) worth of work done in an hour, why wouldn't you do it?

3. Current circumstances predict the future so there's no point in trying.

Where you are now is not a predictor of where you are going to be—that is pure BS (old, limiting **B**elief **S**ystems). Regardless of your circumstances, it is never too late to go for what you want. You can be and do anything you want—NOW. Creating has to come from what is desired vs. what is thought possible. It is possible to quantum leap results through alignment, clarity, and insight. That's what the GEENI System is about...hopefully, you are seeing that by now.

4. Strategies and tactics are more important than intuition.

The outer stuff doesn't work if your inner landscape is misaligned. If you can't connect the dots the way you want internally, your 'transmitter' is broken and cannot broadcast properly to attract what you want.

Additionally, your inner landscape is where your mind lives—what you know, expect, and find familiar will be what you tend to see. By working with intuition to see your energetic landscape, you can identify and resolve distortions, blocks, and limitations. THEN the external tactics and strategies can work properly.

If you follow a practical 'outer' course of action but it is not fueled by clarity of purpose and personal power, it becomes a shell—something hollow without meaning, which is not sustainable. By using intuition to see where you are disconnected or detached from the results you want, and to know who you are and why you're here and why these strategies are needed, you ensure that your inner and outer environments are a match which facilitates and accelerates the result(s).

5. That going for the life you want is selfish.

Being selfish is good for you—it's ultimately what preserves your life. (If you weren't selfish about your life, you would let someone take your life, right?)

Author Ayn Rand wrote that it is both irrational and immoral to act against one's self-interest. Just as a car cannot run without fuel, you cannot give to others what you do not have...if you want to support others in living their best life, you must live your own best life.

Really going for it—your most extraordinary life and business—is the primary way you can give more to others. That's not to say you haven't done your best so far in living the life you want...*but,* if any of this message is resonating in that living your best is selfish, something has not yet 'clicked' for you. Finding that 'click' is a lot easier with intuitive guidance.

6. That you have to be confident to live the life you really want.

Fear always precedes great achievement—it only shows up when someone is in motion (in this case, moving toward what they really want). Confidence (or lack of it) is simply a barometer of fear. Confidence grows through action. Right action is revealed through intuitive guidance.

It does not matter if you have tried and failed. All that is relevant is if you are willing to try again—this time using intuition for inspired clarity and action.

The GEENI System gives people a way to consider their situations, relationships and circumstances in a new way—to transcend the bounds of their reason to live the life they were meant to live. Whatever the situation, there is always a Greater Truth, an Energy, an Environment, a Natural Intelligence and our own Integrity around it; our goal is to explore what 'is' to find next-level growth opportunities.

When you are congruent with your true potential and personal power, you will naturally live bigger, bolder, and happier. You will experience new freedom through right opportunities and relationships that are magnetically attracted to you. Whatever you choose to do to add value to the world through your work will have greater impact. Essentially, you live from your genius instead of your mental constructs.

In summarizing the first E in the GEENI System, sit and reflect on what Energy—yours or that around you—is trying to show you right now. This requires just a few minutes of your time, and it may be helpful to journal or doodle or diagram what comes up in your self-dialogue.

- Is there an Energy thread—or pattern—you want to change?
- Have you experienced this Energy before? What does it look like over time, based on previous experience?
- What is your energetic frame of reference for this situation? Is it valid for this situation?
- How can you view your current situation differently when you consider the Energy of/around it?

- As you look around your life, what is the predominant Energy?
- What Energy are you experiencing that you want(ed)?
- What Energy is happening that you didn't/don't want?
- What Energy is present that you haven't noticed before?
- How can you shift the Energy to support new results?
- What is the significance of your Energy right now? Is it momentary and passing or more long-lasting? Is your Energy flowing or is it stuck?
- What can you do to use Energy more effectively to minimize your current growth opportunity and maximize positive results?
- What systems are needed to help you understand and live your Energy once you understand it?

Simply paying attention to the Energy in, around, and through you and your business can be a game-changer. That being said, let's consider the second *E* in GEENI next.

E Is for Environment

The second "E" in the GEENI System stands for your Environment.

This is where it all started for me. My career started as a Feng Shui practitioner. But before I share more about that, let's talk about the larger concept of environments.

An Environment is something that surrounds you and that you operate in both by choice and involuntarily. For example, your office is usually a choice while having a new cell phone tower erected outside your window is usually not.

When it comes to understanding yourself and supporting your personal clarity, there are two routes you can take . . . one is to constantly experiment with your experiences and the other is to consciously design the Environments around you to stimulate and compel new insights and actions. It's the difference between a furnished office space and one you design yourself—the one you furnish will obviously suit your personal tastes and requirements more closely.

While I tend to defer to physical Environments to explain the concept (given my background as a Feng Shui practitioner), there are several other Environments that you participate in all the time. These Environments weave in, around and through each other so you will usually be in more than one Environment at a time.

In random order, here are some of the core Environments that you need to know about:

Business—why you do what you do, how you package, sell and deliver it, who you work with, how your brand expresses in the market, the systems you use… your business is its own Environment AND reflects you, your values, and your energy.

Relationships—clients, colleagues, peers, friends, family, the people in your networks—the people you know are all mirrors for you and pathways to achieve your goals.

Nature—as the source of all existence, nature is a vitally important Environment that can nurture your spirit fully.

Memetic—the ideas you think, the books you read, the movies you watch… the places where you get ideas and think thoughts is what creates action in your life and business.

Intangible—your relationship with the unseen (faith, spirit, quantum energy, etc.) affects your tangible world.

Physical—your physical Environments are your external body. We will talk more about this one in greater detail because Feng Shui believes it holds the most power in terms of 'programming' your life experience.

Time—when you choose to take action is an Environment. For example, when you get going with your day, what's the first thing you do—check email or read the news or create your to-do list? How you allocate your time is an Environment.

Self—everything about you is an Environment—your feelings, emotions, priorities, perceptions, decisions, health, vitality, thought patterns, language choices, etc.

E IS FOR ENVIRONMENT

As a metaphor, if you were a fish, then your Environments include everything in the tank you swim in, the oxygen you breathe, the carbon filtration system, other fish, the décor, the temperature... anything that affects you in any way is an Environment around you.

The bottom line is that Environments cause results. We are, to a significant degree, a product of our Environments.

One of my clients is an actress and performer and she takes care of herself accordingly—she always looks fit and healthy. I asked her how she could be so disciplined. Her answer was that it wasn't about discipline—it was about knowing she would be able to continue to attract the kinds of jobs she wanted. Her body was her business card/professional Environment. For me, that was mind-blowing at the time.

The point is you can set your Environments up to pull you forward instead of working hard to push yourself from behind. The traditional way to support personal growth was through setting goals, using willpower, discipline, and focus. But what if it could be easy? What if each of your Environments pulled you forward in both intentional ways and unexpected, positive ways? What if you crafted each of them in ways that totally brought out your best—every time? Would life be more interesting or richer or more fun if you made positive changes to your Environments?

To continue our example, your personally-designed office would give you intentional support...now what if you included a high-tech component or a group gathering room or a projector that flashed motivational quotes and images on the wall? These things would create new experiences you never expected, motivate you to try new things and grow in new ways. It's easier to try new things when you are in an Environment that encourages innovation and feel nourished, inspired, and stimulated.

Think about what gives you Energy—watching the news or a movie? Meeting new people or reading a magazine you wouldn't normally read? Eclectic input keeps your brain fresh with new ideas. By refining your Environments to inspire you (either by releasing what doesn't or adding what does), you can literally change the course of your life.

What charges or excites you will be different from other people. What can you do to feel more supported, happy and nourished every day in each of your Environments? Initially, answering that question may bring you some difficult choices, like having overdue conversations, having to move to a new location or even firing clients. However, when your Energy increases and you feel lighter, happier and clearer, it will be worth it.

One of the most interesting and overlooked aspects of Environments is that they are already there—you live in them every day. The idea here is to start using them to your advantage. As you notice things you've not looked at or considered before, you will naturally upgrade your Environments in terms of how you want to experience your results.

Most people get things done despite their Environments; the truth is your Environments help create results. For example, do you think it more probable that you would finish writing your book if you were sitting in the middle of a football field during a game or sitting in a quiet library filled with books to inspire and stimulate your mind?

To develop a collaborative relationship with your Environments and allow them to teach you (vs. you using discipline to make it happen), use the GEENI System to determine the elements you want to upgrade in each Environment. For example, to upgrade your Self Environment, you can ask questions like:

Is it an accurate statement to say that having a green juice right now will add to my energy?

Would the most appropriate use of my time right now be to take a nap?

Is the feeling I am having right now related to something in my business? My personal life?

Is it an accurate statement to say I need to read a book this week? One I have never read? One that is/is not related to business? One that I pick up randomly at a bookstore? The first book that I hear about after this GEENI session?

Keep following the answers you get with questions based on your curiosity to determine where to begin upgrading your Environments.

About Your Feng Shui

Feng Shui, pronounced fung shway, is a 4,000 year-old Chinese art and science based on the understanding that the blend of our own Energy and the vibrations of the Energy in our surroundings—or, our external body—affect the balance we experience in life. This exchange of Energy can have either an inspiring influence to help us actualize our goals, or an overwhelming effect, draining our resources, and putting obstacles in our way.

Take a moment to close your eyes and think of being in your mother's house. Now imagine yourself in your best friend's house. Would you know which one you were in with your eyes covered? Yes—because of how they FEEEEL... THAT is the power of Feng Shui!

The ancient Chinese masters watched how Energy moves through space and time and related that to our experiences here on the physical plane. By shifting your Environment, you shift your life.

According to Chinese legend, there are 5 levels of factors that impact life—heaven-luck and man-made-luck (which we cannot influence), the Environment, philanthropy, and education. This means that Feng Shui, your Environment, is the first place to affect change in your life. In fact, your Feng Shui is more important than being a philanthropist or being educated. Feng Shui is the way to program your life for the outcomes you want. And you're living with your Feng Shui every day now—how amazing will your life and business be when you're creating consciously?

There are four elements to positive and supportive personal Feng Shui: you, your goals, your Environment, and the timing. Please know that there are many schools of Feng Shui; my work and recommendations are based on the tools and techniques of the Black Sect of Tantric Buddhism school (commonly known as "Black Hat" Feng Shui) as founded by Grand Master Lin Yun.

The practice of Feng Shui is much more than fancy interior design; instead, it is infusing your intention into your space and setting the structure of your external body (your environment) in place to help you get what you want. By aligning your personal Energy with your Environment and reflecting that through placing elements, colors, and shapes in "auspicious" positions around you, you can positively influence your wealth, relationships, health, and businesses. Naturally, your ability to achieve your business goals is influenced heavily by your Environments.

Because your Environment is your external body, it can give you very clear clues about what is happening in your inner world. Everything "out there" is a reflection of what's happening "in here." What you see is what you experience, and what you experience is reflected in how you feel.

E IS FOR ENVIRONMENT

On a primal level, we orient ourselves to our place in the world through time and space, so when our Environment is out of order, feels chaotic, or doesn't "flow," it threatens our survival instincts.

That is, if you do not have order in your world, you may find yourself not only unable to function optimally but also to look for the negatives in your world. If that becomes your "norm," you could start to see everything through that filter. And, because humans tend to filter out what we already know (for example, think about driving your car down the street as an example—you don't brake at every distraction), over time, you don't see the chaos anymore. However, just because you can't see it doesn't mean you are not feeling the effects of it!

One of my clients was shaken to learn I knew about her recently impending divorce through her closet. Another client discovered his business couldn't grow through attracting new clients because there was no room left for new client files in the cabinets. (We helped him clean up his files and focus on his existing clients; within three weeks, he landed a $4M policy from someone he'd worked with for years.) Another client learned his intention (mental Environment) to be the general manager over a car dealership was limited to his written words—'over one car dealership'—vs. the regional flagship store and, so, was overlooked for a promotion.

Look around to see what your Environment is showing you right now. If you were a stranger in your space, what do you see? Take your phone out and take pictures of what is around you. Your phone's camera lens will not filter out the familiar so it will capture the 'stuff' you are immune to seeing anymore.

When you see clutter, unfinished projects, piles of stuff or your floor filing system is everywhere, you have clogged environmental arteries. The resulting effect is simple. For example, if your floor is a mess, you are literally creating mountains to climb in your life. By putting stuff in your way, you are creating obstacles in your life that you have to overcome.

Do you have over-stuffed junk drawers?

Are your cabinets well-organized or spilling over?

Do you have shelves bending in the middle from weight?

These all count because it all affects you and your Energy flow.

By looking at your Environment holistically—the clients you work with, the products you develop, the emails you send, the social media you post—you can see whether you feel supported or drained by each aspect of your Environment.

If you feel drained, that is where to begin upgrading your life. You can literally shift your world by clearing out what doesn't serve you anymore. If you don't love it and it doesn't serve a purpose, it needs to be tossed or given to a new home who can love and use it.

To inspire you to work with your Feng Shui, here are a few client stories from my practice.

As mentioned previously, I worked with a 6'2" tall realtor who had a basement office with low ceilings and a small desk—the kind an elementary-age child would do homework on after school. He didn't know why he wasn't attracting new listings. We moved his desk to where he could stand up straight, got him a larger desk that could handle the paperwork of new listings, and added color to his office. Within the first week, he got two new listings.

A manufacturer of a multiple-generation family business could not understand why he didn't have more money in the bank. We looked at his accountant's office and saw there were some problem areas. When I sat in that accountant's desk chair, I felt an odd Energy

E IS FOR ENVIRONMENT

'suck.' We adjusted those challenge areas, then adjusted my client's 'presidential' office for clarity. Within three days, he discovered his long-time accountant had been embezzling for years—the total being in six figures! Within the next few months, he was able to expand his operations with the money he was making and now keeping.

A health food maven wasn't growing her business as quickly as she wanted and was frustrated with all the details she had to handle daily. But her office furniture placement had her in a vulnerable position, with her assistant in the power position in the office. The first thing you saw on entering the office was the paper shredder which was eating up opportunities coming in the door. We reconfigured her office furniture placement and, within two weeks, she gained new speaking opportunities and was happier overall.

An MLM executive had a beachside property on the market for six months without even a nibble. She needed to sell it for her asking price to make her new oceanside home mortgage. She was straddling both deals so she had to sell the first one pronto. We did a release ritual and, within one week, she sold it at her full asking price of $800k.

Here are a few Feng Shui tips you can use to shift your experience starting now.

The front door and your desk are two areas that need to be clean, organized and well-lit. Your desk should be facing your office door but not directly in front of it to be in the command position of the space.

Potential obstacles to positive business flow include: files on the floor (which could be creating obstacles for you to climb over), having your back to the door when seated, gifts from people you don't like or care about, old/former client files having a prominent location, leads just sitting in your inbox, anything that prevents you from working easily, equipment (computer, phone) that is out of date or doesn't work well, objects that reflect who you used to be and not who you are today, energy shredders (paper shredder, paper cutter, nails on walls not being used, harsh overhead light), oe work items in your personal space (especially your bedroom).

The word "clutter" comes from the English word that means 'to clot,' if that helps you understand the importance of this process.

What's in front of you when sitting at your desk is what pulls you forward into your future (or blocks you). What's behind you when sitting at your desk is what gives you (or detracts from) support.

The furthest back left-hand corner from the door is your wealth area. Having flowing water (a fountain, an aquarium) is flowing money. Having symbols of wealth in that area is helpful.

Remember that working with your Environments is a personal process—what works for your best friend may not work for you. And it's relative in that what works in one situation for you may not work in another, or to varying degrees. This is not meant to cause you confusion from the beginning, but rather, to ease the expectations you may have about working with your Environments. You could liken this to cooking your own best recipe—except that you are discovering your own ingredients, in the appropriate ratios with your own mixing process, with the right utensils and your own timing as you go!

As you begin working intentionally with your Environments to achieve more success in your business, it will be important for you to be aware of how and when things shift from what they *were* to what they *become*. One of the hallmarks of being human is we forget a lot of the most painful things once we are out of crisis, and just focus on the result of not being in pain. However, we miss getting our teachings (the wisdom of our lessons) that way—and we miss the celebrations too!

E IS FOR ENVIRONMENT

In summarizing the second E in the GEENI System, sit and reflect on your Environment(s). This requires just a few minutes of your time, and it may be helpful to journal or doodle or diagram what comes up in your self-dialogue.

- What is your current business Environment? Does it feel positive and abundant?
- For a challenge facing you now, what Environment is being compromised or limited?
- Do you like and feel comfortable where you work daily?
- Do you feel nurtured by the Environments around you?
- Is there an energy thread, or pattern, about your Environments you want to change?
- What Environments give you the most positive feelings? Where is your favorite room to work? What about it makes it your favorite?
- How can you view your current Environments differently? Is there something you need to do to upgrade your Environments?
- What conversations have you been putting off that need to be had to clean up a relationship or situation?
- What Environments do you need to release to give you more energy? (This could be anything from relationships to gluten, from watching the news to getting rid of clothes you don't wear anymore.)
- What Environments do you participate in that you don't want? (This could be networking groups, unhealthy eating patterns, not having time for self-care or ???)
- What Environments have you not noticed before that fill you up?
- How can you shift your Environments to support new results?

- What can you do in your current Environments to show up more powerfully and maximize positive results?
- What systems are needed in your Environments to support you in living your truth and help tasks flow more easily?

Simply paying attention to the Environments you are living and working in can give you access to new resources and clarity. That being said, let's consider the *N* in GEENI next.

FREE – Bonus E-Book

Download **"Discover How Your Environment is Translating Messages to Your Unconscious Self for Support OR Sabotage"** as my gift.

Get It NOW at

www.FlowingFengShui.com

N is Your Natural Intelligence

The "N" in the GEENI System is what I call Natural Intelligence. As a professional intuitive, this one is near and dear to me.

Natural Intelligence is the deep wisdom that comes through:

- Source Energy (whatever you call the personal relationship with your higher power),
- your soul's purpose/core energy, and,
- your conscious, authentic truth.

It is your inner acumen, the sage within, the accessible mystic who lives within and through you every day.

When you are in or want to create major transition, your Natural Intelligence is waiting to support you in every way. Your inner guide will never steer you wrong, provided you understand the language of your intuition. And therein lies the key.

You get messages constantly, but social conditioning in the Western world does not allow for your life to be one continuous stream of intuitive thoughts.

Many cultures still heavily rely on Natural Intelligence to help them live a better life. However, you have likely not learned to refer to your right brain because the Industrial Age prized the left brain's A-B-C logical thinking to process in a linear way.

The language of Natural Intelligence is through symbols, messages, colors, repetition, and nature. It speaks through sounds (clairaudience), feelings (clairsentience), and/or pictures (clairvoyance).

While everyone is 'wired' to tap into Natural Intelligence, many people forget they can access this powerful resource anytime.

Here is a quick story from one of my clients about working with her intuition:

> *"Lynn was recommended to me by a dear friend who was experiencing a turnaround after their work together. It took me quite a long time to actually make the call. I'm not sure why, "too busy," I suppose, and it seemed too "woo-woo" to me... life mentor, intuitive, Feng Shui, etc.*
>
> *Well... I finally got desperate enough to make the call. As I write this, things are happening in my life that I never dreamed possible. Lynn is teaching me to have dreams, unabashedly. I never had the courage to open up to the universe, let go and let it flow. Every step of the journey, even when I falter, Lynn reframes everything to the positive, some of which I don't understand at the time but, fortunately, I have come to trust in her processes.*
>
> *There has subsequently been a human chain of incredible people who have come into my life. My personal life has taken off, not in the way I thought it would, but different... and better. My work life is unfolding incredibly, beyond my comprehension. My home is becoming just that—my home—and, for the first time in my life, it's an expression of who I am.*
>
> *I am a high-maintenance woman—ask anyone who knows me. Lynn is always there for me, be it via email, by phone or in person. She allows me to feel like her number one client, but the relationship is egalitarian... we walk side-by-side.*

N IS YOUR NATURAL INTELLIGENCE

I continue to be a piece of work in progress. I am eager to see what the future holds as I walk along my path with Lynn."

~ Betsy Farver, Resource Development Officer

Betsy listened to her Natural Intelligence to get outside perspective to help her shift her experience. That took tremendous courage because she, like most people, was accustomed to more conventional approaches.

Let's make this personal . . . ask yourself the following questions that fly in the face of conventional cultural wisdom but which have the power to create significant change on your terms.

How is Natural Intelligence trying to help you right now?

What message is trying to come through to help you?

Unfortunately, too many people have regrets because of a 'failure to launch' when it comes to living their best, most fulfilling, most extraordinary life. They get complacent where they are and forget they have choices. They don't remember what it means to allow Natural Intelligence to guide them.

"The most beautiful thing we can experience is the mysterious. It is the source of all true art and science."

~ Albert Einstein

Imagine what it would be like to know your true essential self and to live from that place—that place which is SO amazing, inspired, and effortless that it's painful to live anywhere else (or have anything less as an Environment)?

What would it be like if you knew you could break through the B.S. (Belief Systems) that keep you living 'less than' results and live from the power of your energy?

What if you get to the end of your life and look back with regret on the things you didn't do because of fear, analysis paralysis, confusion, distraction, or overwhelm? If that were the case, you are basically saying all those self-perceived limitations are bigger than you are in your own life—and that's just not possible when you live in alignment with Natural Intelligence.

What would it look like if your business supported you in holistic problem solving, surviving predictable deluges, using your natural resources in new ways, being a commuter route for your clients to achieve new results, and becoming a thriving, long-lasting part of the very fabric of your industry?

When you know how your Natural Intelligence is communicating with you AND you cultivate that connection, clarity is the only natural outcome.

9 Secrets to Creating Positive Change Through Natural Intelligence

As an entrepreneur, business owner, freelance professional, or consultant, it's likely you want to make the world a better place. And you also likely know it starts with you. As you evolve, your business evolves, and so you make a bigger, "cleaner" contribution and the world benefits. You have big dreams. It's through those dreams and your personal transformation that you have the power to make the world a better place.

By working with Natural Intelligence to create positive change for yourself, you are acknowledging your power as a creator and being accountable for your Energy (and results of it). In random order, here are nine secrets to creating positive change and transforming the world through Natural Intelligence.

1. Align with what feels right for you.

If it doesn't make sense for you, it's not yours—even if that's "what everybody else is doing" (or maybe especially if that's the case!). Use no one else's measurement in determining your goals nor your progress. When you follow Natural Intelligence and are aligned with what is right for you, you resonate at the highest vibration for you—and *that* creates positive change in exponential ways.

2. Finish old business or let it go.

If you haven't gotten to something on your "to-do" list for a long time, decide if it's really something you are supposed to get done. If yes, do it. If not, get it off your list (and, if need be, you can create a "parking lot" of those ideas for some future revisiting). The idea is to free up the mindspace those projects are holding and release you from beating yourself up for not getting them done. That's valuable energy you can use to create positive change vs. staying focused on the past. We live in an abundant world. Natural Intelligence doesn't want you to play small or feel guilty.

3. Accept responsibility for what you create.

And that means pretty much everything... if you aren't the cause of your life, you are the effect of it which puts you in reaction to your life and makes you a victim on some level.

To be a creator, you must own what you've created so you give yourself the power to create your future. If you don't know what your responsibility was, track back to where you own your result (example: the airline lost your luggage—you "own" that occurrence because you chose to travel in the first place or chose that airline or chose a plain black suitcase or... or... or...). Your Natural Intelligence is always waiting to give you insights and options.

4. Receive what comes in.

Be open and willing to accept what comes to you because you asked for and created it. By limiting, negating, or rejecting what comes into your life, you are constricting the flow and emitting confusing energy as to what you want. If what you receive isn't what you expected, go back to your point of creation *or* make a fresh intention with this new information as a guide. Be sure to check in with your Natural Intelligence about any point of confusion in your request or the situation for insight.

5. Don't judge yourself for what was or the decisions you made in the past.

If you would have known better, you would have done better then (and that goes for the rest of us too!). Generally, you are your own worst critic and say things to yourself you would never say out loud to another person. Show yourself the same kindness you would show a stranger and watch the positive change as it happens in your life and business. Your Natural Intelligence does not judge—it will only work from the information at hand to create what's coming next.

6. Know you are provided for by the Universe.

Source Energy does not let your good work go unrewarded. Creating positive change is an action and an energy that becomes attractive for new opportunities, relationships, and resources. Trust yourself, and Source, that you are always provided for, even (or especially) during a significant positive transformation cycle.

If you need proof that Source has your back, well . . . you're reading this now, right? You have made it through some terrible times and you're still standing. That's Natural Intelligence in action.

7. Upgrade your Energy sources.

A Gulfstream 7 airplane doesn't run on diesel fuel . . . an animal doesn't do well after drinking from a poisoned pond . . . and neither does your positive change. Look around your world to see what is supporting you, and make sure it really *is* supporting you! Maybe it has outlived its time, or you have different needs, or something has shifted—if this is the case, it's time for a release and/or replacement. Upgrade your sources of energy, using Natural Intelligence as your guide, to support your optimal flow for positive change.

8. Forget perfection.

If you are attached to being perfect before something can happen, or that something else has to be perfect before you can benefit, or that there are negative consequences when something isn't perfect, you can severely limit your positive change. Change can be messy in the middle—it's hard to be perfect when renovating a house! Your Natural Intelligence always has your back so everything will work out in the end. For example, think of all the pictures taken of you when you thought you were fat at the time—in looking back, now you see that you were actually lookin' pretty good, right? Be in the flow of change and know imperfect is, really, pretty perfect.

9. Detach from the form in which 'it' arrives.

If you expect roses in a long, rectangular box, and you get a hand-painted postcard with a rose on it and are disappointed, you're probably going to have a hard time recognizing and receiving your positive change when it happens. By setting your intention through your Natural Intelligence, and then letting go of what it needs to look like, you are giving it the ultimate freedom to be what it needs to be . . . and sometimes that is even more spectacular positive change than you could have dreamed of for yourself.

One more point to consider... if you experience what feels like 'rejection' on any level, know that is Natural Intelligence running interference for you. It means the opportunity, circumstance, or relationship is not for you and there is something better available—even if you can't see it yet.

At any rate, your awareness of your own positive transformation process means you are being of the highest service in making the world a better place. So, make the world better, help a lot of people, and create a big huge global shift by starting where it counts—with yourself.

Go Beyond Your Reason

You cannot get beyond the bounds of your own reason (what you believe is true) to create something dramatically different.

However, the GEENI System helps you identify what has kept you small. Even if you have tried and failed before, the GEENI System can get under the surface view so you can get fresh insight to make new decisions and accelerate your results.

The answers are within you but you (like all of us!) can't see them on your own—think of an eye trying to see itself. That's where the GEENI system comes in to help by giving you a way to understand the language of your Natural Intelligence as well as cultivate a clearer connection with it.

To be even more proactive in receiving your messages with clarity, you can take steps to raise your energetic vibration. This means such things as: focusing on the positive in every situation, being aware of and choosing the words you use to communicate carefully, honoring your boundaries, living your truth, taking care of your business (emotional, spiritual, mental, physical, etc.) and letting others take care of theirs. (This process alone could be a book!) ;+)

Something I am seeing is an emerging breed of entrepreneur who rides the wave of intrinsic motivation, dancing with the fire burning in their belly to change the world by expressing who they are and what they came to do at an essential level. They get paid almost as a by-product because money is fuel—not motivation.

Until now, conventional business has been focused on strategies, techniques, tactics, systems and 'follow me' boxes of 'you can do it this way too.' Business is 'noisy' with people shouting about their wares, pounding their message relentlessly while competing against each other with the same factors (usually price in the same customer pool).

And yet, silent awareness is the path of greater success as proven through time, nature, and those masters who have gone before us. Silence is the cosmic breath that breathes through to inspire and activate authentic power.

In the midst of that profound space for insight, your role is to practice discernment by communing with your Natural Intelligence to interpret and then express wisdom.

In other words, the leading edge of business is to go with what you know vs. what you are told (or even believe).

- Explore the edge of your industry with fresh perspective and a willingness to see what is unknown, unfamiliar and unexpected.
- Let go of what doesn't serve you even if you don't yet have the resources you think you need for what you want to do.
- Partner with others in new ways for win-win-win scenarios (your partner, you *and* your customers).

Essentially, being in business today means building a business beyond reason which happens when you allow Natural Intelligence to guide you. Following are some signs of business beyond reason.

- **Wall clock time**
  It is unreasonable to build a great business that changes the world on a 9–5 schedule. Truly great achievements happen through a flow state and, even more, fueled with the intention of doing something good for others.

- **Hard and soft**
  It is counterintuitive to be 'hard' and 'soft' at the same time. To set boundaries, stick to structure and follow best business practices *and* still be open and vulnerable to receive Energy, participate in relationships and maintain a sense of wonder is not easy but it is necessary.

- **Unique as one**
  It is uncomfortable to promote your uniqueness when in a state of wisdom because you recognize we are all one. So how do you presume to stand out—to be seen—as an individual for success in business?

- **Infobesity**
  It is overwhelming to stay current with the information now available in the marketplace. It's been said that one Sunday edition of The Wall Street Journal represents the sum of knowledge available to a person over a lifetime when Thomas Jefferson lived.

- **Same but different**
  It is challenging to surrender to the wisdom of being who you are in the context of a world who wants you to be the same and yet needs you to be different.

Entrepreneurial transformation is the process of going beyond the bounds of your comfort zone, beyond what others expect, beyond what seems reasonable to truly move and transform people in a meaningful, singular, and significant way through your business. Natural Intelligence is the modality by which to do so with ease and clarity.

I'll teach more on that by sharing my own story...

There was a time when I thought I had to follow other people's rules to be successful and that my 'elders' would tell me what was most valuable about me to set up my business (which they didn't/couldn't—I had to decide that). I was petrified to start a business—who was I to be an entrepreneur? What if I didn't do it right? What if people didn't like me or my business?

And yet, I was compelled to help others and to receive payment for doing so. I sat in my cubicle jobs and was miserable, thinking of the time I was wasting when I could be doing so much more. Being good at whatever task I was assigned, I was over-utilized, over-responsible and under-appreciated. All I could think is that I was building someone else's dream instead of my own, and not helping others where I could have done so much more with that time.

Eventually, I had my full-time jobs 'on the side' while I jumped into business endeavors the rest of my waking hours. In the beginning, there were projects that went horribly awry, frustration at not knowing what I didn't know and unexpected conversations I had to lead to sort out sticky situations. It was awful. But I couldn't stop—business was in my blood. And I *knew* there was more for me through business.

By 1998, I had started working for a dot com that became a dot bomb. I was 'given my freedom' (let go from a job) on December 15 of that year—it was devastating. And it was one of the most significant turning points of my life because it was then I determined I would not be a leaf on someone else's tree; instead, I would be my own tree. I had to go beyond what I thought was reasonable, based on everyone else's opinion, to build a business on my true gifts. At the time, people thought I was nuts.

Since that moment, through times thick and thin, the one thing that has kept my inner fire going (then and now) is the knowing that I had something special to offer people and I wanted to help them. I know my connection with Natural Intelligence is unwavering. And that was enough to get me through scarcity, debt, fear, distraction, loneliness, being ahead of my time, friends and family judging me, moving from state to state, wandering around while I figured it all out, watching others succeed while it seemed I was stuck in my wandering.

I studied, took training, hired mentors, went to seminars, watched webinars, read books, participated in masterminds, attended events, listened to teleseminars, did research online...you name it and I was integrating it. Without even really knowing it, my business morphed along with me. Fortunately, I had named my business so it could grow with me. And, without really knowing it, I became more present to myself, my reputation as a teacher grew and my income climbed.

Long story short, I took the scenic route to success. It took me *years* to sort out and package my talent. Along the way, I added some important skills that have benefitted not just me but my (then future) clients as well. In the end, had I been myself in the first place, I see now that I would have had a very different (and, frankly, likely more lucrative) experience.

As a result, I am devoted to accelerating success through Natural Intelligence, my wisdom, and hard-earned experience for innovators, change agents, and visionary entrepreneurs so they can reach their potential, help more people, and change the world more easily through their work.

Naked Intelligence

When the wisdom of Natural Intelligence shows up, it's not fancy. It doesn't judge you. It doesn't speak in intellectual terms. It can transcend your senses, override your will, and be something you just 'know' in your cells. It isn't packaged to be pretty and, yet, the naked clarity is what is compelling about it.

Natural Intelligence is specific, although you may have to learn how it communicates with you. It isn't about words as much as it is about knowingness. It defies description—how can you describe the taste of chocolate to someone who has not yet had chocolate? However, once you tune into it, it changes how you perceive everything.

The wisdom you receive quiets the questions. And it is the fastest path to freedom, in my opinion.

Freedom means not having something external make your decisions for you. It means not allowing material goods to own you. It means taking on the mantle of responsibility that comes with exercising independence in alignment with Natural Intelligence and in service to the greater good.

When you are free, you claim purposeful sovereignty in your life and you willingly accept that you must show up in congruent accountability for who you came here to be—in all areas of your life.

The myth is that freedom means a free ride on roads paved with gold. The truth is that freedom is something you earn every day through your thoughts, words and actions.

To find your freedom, here's a simple formula:

Stop doing what doesn't serve you and start doing what does.
You can know what that is by referencing your Natural Intelligence.

According to Lori Barr, M.D., most people believe making that kind of change starts with action; however, this belief actually sabotages people from achieving what they desire—because action is the *result* of their inner wisdom—and so they slink away from their goals in dejected failure.

Doing something different, like finding new freedom, begins by asking your Natural Intelligence what it is you are to do next. As you get answers, you begin having sensations and then an emotion about them. An emotion is a noun while a feeling is a verb—and they are very different experiences. An emotion can be quantified while a feeling is more subjective.

The sensation of Natural Intelligence moving through you will be captured by your mind as an emotion to quantify the experience and give it words (ideally, using conscious language—present tense, positive, powerful). Only when you've been through these stages—connecting to your Natural Intelligence, feeling the sensation, surfacing it as an emotion and then assigning it conscious language—can you begin to take effective action.

NOW you can make decisions to express what has come through inspiration (or, 'in spirit action').

Action without the back-up of clarity is like walking out the door to head to a foreign country without knowing why you're going or what to take with you, much less having a map or a language translator.

As you begin to act in alignment with Natural Intelligence, your experiences are going to be different than ever before in your life. Why? Because you have stopped what didn't work and are following guidance in a new way. You are empowering your awareness to assign meaning to what you're doing because that is what anchors spiritual consciousness in your physical world.

And THAT is freedom.

When you're in that place of sacred liberty, everything else—even things that you would typically think of as obstacles or learning points—well, it all pales in comparison. It doesn't matter that you have to learn how to do bookkeeping, or study marketing, or go beyond your comfort zone in learning technology...those are necessary learning opportunities that allow you to activate your potential, express your essence, and accelerate your results.

When you are prepared, you are 'lucky'...things fall into place because you seem to magnetize, recognize and optimize opportunities. In reality, that means cultivating your strengths, building your skills, and having resilience in whatever happens...trusting the bigger picture you've been invited to convey as a conduit for universal Energy...being willing to do what needs to be done as it pulls you forward.

Again, that is freedom...and it's not the 'oh, I can do anything I want' kind of freedom many people think of (especially the people who have jobs and don't understand what you're doing in your business...). Instead, when you are honoring freedom and being of sincere contribution, you are rewarded with moments of absolute rapture. You do get to experience things other people can't...because you were willing to do what most people won't do (whatever their reason).

Ironically, to experience freedom means being willing to start at the beginning, to show up again and again for the wisdom teaching of the day through your Natural Intelligence, and consciously grow yourself on every level because you have chosen to hear the message to make a difference in your unique way.

Never in history have we had this level of not only permission but responsibility—and even calling—to honor freedom in its highest form. Honoring freedom is about following through on what's right for you, made known by your Natural Intelligence, because then you and everyone you touch will benefit from your clarity, commitment, and contribution.

In summarizing the N in the GEENI System, sit and reflect on what Natural Intelligence is communicating to you. This requires just a few minutes of your time, and it may be helpful to journal or doodle or diagram what comes up in your self-dialogue.

- What is your current business Environment? Does it feel positive and abundant?
- Do you know what your Natural Intelligence is saying to you? Is there a message about your business?
- Do you have the business you want? If not, why not? What is standing in the way?
- Are you honoring boundaries both for yourself and your business?
- For a challenge facing you now, what is your Natural Intelligence saying for a next-step action?
- When your Natural Intelligence is communicating with you, does it come through in words, sensations, emotions, pictures or something else?
- Do you feel connected with your Natural Intelligence? How can you connect more deeply with your Natural Intelligence?
- Is there a pattern to the insights you gain from your Natural Intelligence?
- What is the best set-up to gain insights from your Natural Intelligence? Do you need to be in nature or in your office? Do you need quiet or meditation music? Does your connection feel strong enough that you can get messages anytime you need/want them?
- What do you need to do to get your messages with greater clarity? Is there something you need to do to increase your vibration? Or do you simply need to practice getting your messages?

- What messages or knowingness have you already received that still need action to be resolved?
- What insights would, if you had them, be the most beneficial to you now? If you can answer this question, use these desired insights as the starting place to connect with your Natural Intelligence.
- What messages do you get that you don't want? And what do you do with them? In the past, what has happened when you ignored them?
- What Natural Intelligence messages or insights have you not noticed before that feel good and give you strength?
- What can you do to use your Natural Intelligence to show up more powerfully and maximize positive results?
- What systems do you need to put in place to access and then apply the wisdom, messages and insights that come from your Natural Intelligence?

Your Natural Intelligence is always accessible and is always helping you get to your next-best level—especially when it doesn't seem like it! When you have clarity around what that looks like in the bigger picture, it's easier to step into uncomfortable places for greater clarity, freedom and aligned results.

That being said, let's consider the *I* in GEENI as the final step in the GEENI System.

I Stands for Integrity

This next (and final) step is about the infamous "I" in the GEENI System, which stands for Integrity. As in, what's up with your personal alignment?

You can only create and manifest intentional change when you are lined up in every way—when there is Integrity between who you are, what you do, and how you show up in the world.

You might think integrity means you are honest, which is one definition. However, the definition we will be working is the one that references the strength or condition of being. Just as a ship's hull requires Integrity to be waterproof and strong against the powerful and ever-changing force of water, you need to have Integrity in your life and business to be able to navigate the rigors of living it.

Here are some of the qualities and characteristics that define Integrity:

- The state of being whole and undivided
- Firm adherence to a code of especially moral or artistic values (aka, incorruptible)
- An unimpaired condition (aka, being of 'sound' mind, body or state)
- The quality or state of being complete
- Expressing clearly aligned focus between thoughts and words, words and actions, beliefs and behaviors.

For our purposes, that means you must be in Integrity with yourself, your life purpose, your Energy, your Environment, your relationships, your health, your money, your business systems—everything.

It's easy to see those times in life when you haven't had Integrity. Think back to a moment when you were suffering the results of a bad decision made impulsively, based on peer pressure, or on what someone else needed instead of on what you knew to be true. That would be the most basic reminder of how necessary it is to be in Integrity—to avoid pain.

Beyond that, when you are in Integrity, things flow easier, people and opportunities are drawn to you, and you're happier and more optimistic. Integrity brings everything together seamlessly, easily, and nearly effortlessly when you're living it.

According to my client Bill Ipsan, Credit Advisor:

> *"Ms. Scheurell has given me great insight to another dimension of life. She is part of my balance team to deal with life's increasing challenges. With her mentoring, I am able to view life through another dimension and can add my decision-making process to what is more than language, thought or intellect."*

Integrity is about making decisions in alignment with who you are even with the external pressures of daily life and when nobody's looking. For clues on how integrity does—or doesn't—show up in your life, it's time to go underneath to the roots of your integrity system.

Think back to your childhood—consider your "programming" around integrity.

- Were you encouraged to be on time to school?

- Were you supported in telling the truth?
- Did you try to get your homework done completely before class?
- Did you participate fully in everything you did?
- Did you make sincere friends with people you could take with you your whole life?

The keys to your Integrity today can be found in your childhood. If you find your Integrity is compromised, it's time to take ownership and reprogram your internal Integrity paradigms with what you know today.

Follow, speak and act from your truth and you will be in Integrity.

Integrity Is the Glue for Sustainable Success

Togetherness is a beautiful thing... that statement is all about Integrity. Integrity is the glue which creates synergy between who you are and how your business is expressing, as well as what your customers expect, and how you deliver on that promise. It's a big deal.

Integrity in business is about congruence of thought, word, and behavior. You say what you mean, mean what you say, and do what you say. Integrity is what can make or break your business success, even if it is an unconscious process.

If you aren't clear on where your integrity is lacking, your business is paying the price by not attracting reliable clients or even losing clients, leaving money on the table, and experiencing "unexpected" (aka, undesirable) results. In fact, start understanding what is happening with your Integrity by looking at those scenarios where you are not getting the results you expect.

When you know the hallmarks of positive Integrity, who you are is evident, your business is a clear expression of your intention and purpose, and potential and current customers are magnetically drawn to you ensuring your business success over time.

The Language of Integrity

Unfortunately, you (like all of us) have experienced the opposite, or lack, of Integrity at some point with people who have broken promises to you, or situations that turned out different from their marketing and promotions, or vendors who didn't deliver as they said they would when you purchased from them. They do not inspire your trust or confidence. And you probably did not choose to do business with them as a result.

Following are examples of how Integrity shows up—or not—through business. If you are not in Integrity:

- Your word will be meaningless.
- You might engage in gossip or negativity in conversation.
- You aren't concerned with the value people receive—only that you're putting something out there.
- You do things you don't believe in.
- Your systems are faulty or not on track.
- You don't follow through on your promises.
- You focus on the transaction rather than the client.
- You design products as bread crumb trails rather than complete solutions.
- Your marketing is hype-y and filled with hyperbole and false urgency.
- You do what's easy in the moment instead of what's right in the long run.

- You ignore the Energy and don't pay attention to what's actually happening.
- You are likely attracting lower vibration people, opportunities, and Environments, as well as leaving money on the table.

A lack of Integrity damages your credibility (with yourself and others), sets the stage for distrust going forward, and feels repellant. When your life has a lack of Integrity, multiply the negative consequences by a factor of 10—because it will create 10 times the negativity for you when you create, allow, or accept a lack of Integrity in your life.

If someone makes an honest mistake, that's a different issue. That can be handled with communication, an apology, a new plan. However, if there is a true lack of Integrity based on attitude, previous history, or greater circumstances, that is a different scenario entirely.

> *"The difficulty we have in accepting responsibility for our behavior lies in the desire to avoid the pain of the consequences of that behavior."*
>
> ~ M. Scott Peck

When you are in Integrity:
- You say what you mean and you mean what you say.
- You deliver quality value to your clients and ensure they have received it.
- Your marketing is based on truth.
- Your systems don't have cracks in them where people can get lost.
- You follow through on what you initiate.
- You return phone calls and emails.
- You admit when you're wrong.
- You cultivate real relationships (instead of focusing on what you can get from someone).

- You design products to deliver maximum value (rather than holding back or metering out solutions).
- You live according to your principles (instead of doing something you don't believe).
- You follow the Energy (vs. forcing something to happen).

Some of the hallmarks of Integrity include when:

- You feel the 'click' of things as they flow easily.
- You aren't in resistance or rebellion to new information or behaviors.
- You feel solid when you speak about and through your business.
- Your marketing is real and truthful.
- You have real relationships with your clients.
- You care about the results you deliver (even though you can't be responsible for what people do with what you provide, you can make sure you're adapting to make it optimally consumable).
- Your systems aren't glitchy, require hoops and adapt as needed.
- You feel good about what you do every day—*and* at the end of each day.
- You don't feel drained or guilty about your pricing.
- You can speak about what you do easily with anyone who asks about it.

In the largest sense, your Integrity is the tie that binds you and your experiences in life and business. Essentially, Integrity means strength and solidarity. When you are congruent and aligned with your values, beliefs, thoughts, words, and behavior, you have less (or even no) stress in your life because you are fully expressing yourself. Even more, people will be drawn to your clarity and presence. Look for the areas in your life that are experiencing stress and you will find your invitations to step into greater Integrity.

Life is an echo—what you put out is what you get back. That is decidedly true in the relationships in your life. You can see who you were at different points in your life based on who you attracted into it then.

When you live from your own Integrity, you speak your truth and show up without hesitation. You will also feel centered enough in yourself to ensure your emotional needs are met so that you do not project them on to other people.

In other words, when you have Integrity, you are responsible with your Energy. As a result, you experience cleaner and more fulfilling relationships. Consider any conversations you need to have and just get them done—it will get things back on track with the people in your life.

When you're feeling strong and healthy, it's easier to follow through on everything in your life. When you are in Integrity in your own self-care, you are unstoppable. Take the time to assess how you feel in your body. If there is anything that is unbalanced (and you will know what that is), make plans to address it starting now. If your body wants better nutrition or to move more, you can do that right away. Your Integrity to yourself is the key to living a good life—why throw that away with bad habits, unaddressed issues, neglect or just being lazy? Love yourself enough to be disciplined in how you care for yourself and your life will pay you back for it.

You cannot attract that which is not part of your Energy field—this is the state of being in Integrity. Whatever you are aligned with is what you experience. What you are is what you attract—it cannot be any other way. And that includes abundance in all forms—money, prosperity, good friends, opportunities, etc.

So, when you want to make more money, increase your Integrity around it. Make sure you have a budget, you know your debts, have a pay-off plan, pay your bills on time, and are responsible with your money. If your money were your friend, are you honoring it right now? Get into Integrity around your finances and watch them grow.

It's a New Age

We are now in the Age of Aquarius, which is the astrological sign that connotes knowledge, revolution, and synthesis (or coming together) of systems. The stage for breakthroughs and self-realization is now set. Period.

Naturally, this applies to the Integrity of your life and business. This means that...

Whatever you are tolerating (putting up with) can be no more, whether that's relationships, lifestyle, occupation, or environment. Whatever changes need to be made for your optimal health and wellness are in motion whether you're ready or not. Anything that is out of alignment with Integrity in your life will be revealed to be consciously addressed. Congruence between the inner and outer *will* be achieved.

What you focus your attention on is critical to what you are creating in your life and work like never before—you will manifest the deepest point of your focus. Clarity of perception is undeniable. You will be able to see dynamics, distortions and discoveries without effort.

In other words, the Age of Aquarius is a revolution in consciousness. You, and only you, are completely responsible for your life experience. And it requires you to show up in Integrity in every way. To help acclimate to this new level of consciousness, here are three things you can do now.

ONE: Be accountable to yourself.

- What projects have you put off?
- What projects need to be completed?
- What loose ends are plaguing you?
- What relationships require greater attention and integrity from you?
- What is unsaid for which you are the messenger?
- What are you tolerating in your life and work?
- What needs are you not meeting for yourself?

Now is the time for radical self-honesty. While it will shake up your world, it will make the shift easier because you're confronting it rather than reacting to it.

TWO: Express your dreams.

If there is something you want to know, do, be or experience, now is the time to express it. If your life, including health, relationships, work, isn't what you want it to be, what do you need to do differently?

This isn't about anyone but you—identify and articulate your dreams to start taking action on living them.

THREE: Understand what you are here to do.

You are unique in the fabric of time and space; you are here to contribute something valuable. Chances are that having your own business allows you the space and freedom to do it. The truth is your unique purpose is probably already expressing somewhere in your world whether or not you are an entrepreneur.

In any case, get clarity on what you are here to do and teach in the largest sense so you can do it consciously.

Fair warning: if you do not step into your life with total Integrity and make your distinct contribution, whatever that is, there will be a tsunami wave that will sweep through your life to release what you haven't yet addressed. And that's a lot more traumatic than doing it on your own proactively.

If you feel like every time you turn around that there's something else that requires a new level of attention, that's because there is—life is speeding up. It may feel like you're being squished in the Tectonic plates of your life.

In the moment, that can be a bit overwhelming but, in the end, doing the work now to align all the aspects of your life with Integrity will make things flow easier and with greater intentional result for you in the long run.

Let's consider Integrity more specifically as applied to various areas of your life and work next.

Body

Many people assume they know how to take care of their body because they've been living in it a long time. However, most of what we were taught even a generation ago is no longer considered 'best practices' for healthy, vital living.

Not only have nutritional standards been upgraded, but so have the paradigms around exercise, rest, and meditation. Beyond that, each body is now considered unique in terms of what it needs—from minerals to hormones, blood type to metabolism, your body is its own ecosystem. And it's up to you to figure out what makes it run best.

The human body is designed to live for something like 200+ years but our life choices wear it out early. With proper care and feeding, you can live happier physically for a longer time now.

What does Integrity with your body look like? Having consistent routines for everything from brushing and flossing your teeth to visiting the dentist, from eating every three hours to resting when you're tired and sleeping for at least six hours a night gives your body the structural, nutritional, and active habits that keep you lean and your Energy clean.

Be honest and consider where you are out of Integrity with your relationship with your body. Then don't beat yourself up! Simply commit to new behaviors that honor your body as the vehicle which gets you through life every day.

Personal

The bigger message of being aware of the degree of your Integrity can change everything for you. Once you recognize nothing is too small to be consciously aligned with the best version of yourself, you cannot just toss off a glib comment or procrastinate on a commitment.

The reality is that when you are lacking Integrity in one part of your life, it's also showing up in at least one other area of your life. That means if you are late to meet a friend for drinks, you're likely late for other appointments too—and maybe even work. If you are breaking promises to others, you're breaking promises to yourself. And that does not set you up for success on any level.

When you decide to pay attention to how you're showing up in your life, you give yourself the gift of strength. Integrity is what strengthens all the aspects of your life, bringing them together as mirror aspects of their source—you.

The other aspect of Integrity we need to address here is honesty. That is, do you speak your truth? Are you scrupulous about your standards of conduct so that people can rely on you and they know it? Do you keep your word when you give it?

Having the courage to be honest with yourself and others gives you a greater capacity to have profound connections with others. People know when you're holding out, have expectations, are projecting your stuff and aren't showing up in your full potential. Naturally, in such cases, it's hard to trust you. However, when you are honest and demonstrate Integrity in every area of your life, you naturally attract people's trust as the foundation for cultivating great relationships.

Environment

As you already know, your Environment reflects your inner world. That is, what's 'out there' is 'in here' and vice-versa. So, if you look around at your Environment and it doesn't match who you think you are, it's time to shake things up a bit.

The Environment around you should be clean, functional, attractive and comfortable for you. It should be a mirror of your interests, hobbies, personality and lifestyle. When it isn't, either you've outgrown your Environment or one of you needs an upgrade. ;+)

When it comes to evaluating the Integrity of your space, begin with the biggest concept and work your way down to the specific as follows:

- Is your office located in the right geographical area?
- Is your office in the right type of structure?
- Is the exterior of your office attractive and welcoming for you?
- Is the interior layout of your office conducive to the flow of your business?
- Is the décor attractive? Does the style suit you?
- Do you like the feeling and functionality of the furnishings in the room(s)?

- Is there anything you would change about your furnishings, furniture or artwork?
- Do you have clutter in any room? And, if yes, can you take care of it in less than an hour? (If yes, get it scheduled on your calendar and get it done!)
- Is there anything that needs to be repaired or replaced? If yes, make that a priority.

When you are in Integrity with your Environment, and your Environment is in Integrity with supporting your best life, you will notice that shifts happen. The reason for that is because your Environment is your outer body—as you take care of it, it will take care of you.

Your life needs a physical container to allow you to restore yourself so you can go out and make your contribution in the world. Make sure it's the best container you can create right now—then watch for synchronicities that show you that your desires are being manifested.

Business / Career

When you choose to invest your productivity, it must be congruent with what you care about as well as your unique talents and strengths. Why? Because if you are doing something you don't care about or that you aren't strong in, you are doing it only for the money—and that's not enough to truly motivate you to show up fully. It's also not the way to know that you're making a meaningful difference in the world.

Your work needs to be in Integrity with who you are, what you're good at, and where you want to make a bigger difference. When you commit to being in Integrity through your work, your business, position and/or job will take on a fresh flavor for greater performance and personal fulfillment.

If you are not contributing to something greater than you while using your natural talents, you are stunting yourself. If you are not in the right career, handling the right kinds of responsibilities for the right clients or employer, it will cause you stress and, more than likely, problems at work.

If you are in the right place doing the right things with the right clients or employer situation, the next question becomes: are you showing up fully in Integrity with what you know you can do? If you are holding back, find yourself complaining, or looking for a new career option, you are out of Integrity in your career.

When you get into Integrity with your business/career, you are naturally motivated to add to your skills set, go further on a project and like to take on new responsibilities because you know you are making a significant difference. Let now be the time when you assess the degree of Integrity between your professional life and your personal desires and talents and, where there is a gap, acknowledge it and take action to close it.

Health

> *"When health is absent, wisdom cannot reveal itself, art cannot manifest, strength cannot fight, wealth becomes useless, and intelligence cannot be applied."*
>
> ~ Herophilus

When you are incongruent, or out of Integrity, in any part of your life, your body will experience dis-ease (either in terms of stress or through illness). It is a foundational energy loss because, as you sense you are making choices that don't support your best and highest self, it becomes an energetic drag. In turn, that creates an unnecessary waste of mental Energy.

If you think of a large backpack full of the things you are lacking Integrity with sitting heavily on your back throughout your day, you can imagine the relief of removing that backpack and the Energy that would return for other things in your life. When you have Integrity with your personal goals and choices, you create the conditions for optimal life force Energy through your health.

Being out of Integrity leads to stress and stress is the #1 cause of most illnesses today. You know what you need to do to take care of your health. If you're not doing it, it's time to get honest and consider the greater pay-off you're having from not taking care of yourself. Clearly there is something that is preventing you from honoring yourself, which causes fundamental stress, which takes a toll on your health. Once you identify that root cause for your behavior, you give yourself new options for better health.

In case you are experiencing a lack of optimal health right now, there is a bigger message for you in that experience. It's inviting you to look beyond the symptoms to see what's really going on and make some changes in your life. Your health is the barometer of how you're handling stress, how effectively you're restoring your Energy, and the sum of all the little energy drains that can happen over the course of daily living. Pay attention to get into Integrity so you can enjoy more vital health every day.

Relationships

Your relationships are a match to the Energy you are putting out. When you are in Integrity, congruent with your beliefs and values, speaking your truth and showing up fully to participate in a relationship by taking ownership of your own emotional wellness, your relationships are more engaging and fulfilling.

However, when you are out of Integrity in your relationships (including the one you have with yourself), you set the stage for misunderstandings, miscommunications, and missed opportunities. Ironically, this is the time when you can most grow from your relationships because these are your disguised invitations for growth.

Over time, your relationships will change; in fact, they must, to keep up with your evolution. When you find you have 'unfinished business' with a relationship or past occurrence with another person, it keeps you out of Integrity which will affect other areas of your life.

It is vital you feel supported by your relationships, whether with family, a significant other, a best friend, social circle, colleagues, vendors ... anyone in your world has some relationship with you because they are in your world. You can see how you are showing up by observing who is entering your world and how your relationships are changing.

People who have poor boundaries often struggle in relationships. This is a symptom of poor Integrity with self because boundaries are not honored by others—they are taught to others by how we treat ourselves. When you honor your boundaries, so can others. When you don't know how to honor your boundaries, most people find it easier to sacrifice the relationship than to grow themselves with Integrity and 'own' their part in the relationship dynamic.

In short, consider your relationships and ask yourself how you feel about each one. Notice whether you feel good more than not after seeing that person, if you are participating fully in the relationship, or if you are holding back in some way. Notice what fulfills you and what doesn't, then take action to see your needs get met. That may occur through clear communication and making a request, or it may be through attracting a new relationship. Whatever the relationship, come from a place of Integrity to allow each of you to show up in your full capacity—the key to the most rewarding kind of relationship regardless of the type.

Creativity

When your life is in Integrity with your values, beliefs, thoughts and behaviors, you have more Energy. Your desire to create something new increases and, without the stress of managing incongruence, you feel lighter so you have the Energy to do it. With expansive space in your Energy field, your creativity begins to express itself in new ways.

Creativity is not limited to the arts (painting, music, etc.). Creativity is in how you see the world, the way you approach solving problems, the perspective you have on your relationships as you see with fresh eyes. Life is more spontaneous and you enjoy new freedom in every way—including your creativity.

Interestingly, the best creativity happens when you assign Integrity to it. For example, if you wanted to create (write) a new book, the best way to make that happen is to give yourself deadlines. Why? Because if you don't, you'll never have a sense of urgency to do it.

Your creativity will benefit by having Integrity in how you approach it and the parameters you use to create an actual outcome. And you may decide to not have an outcome—instead, you may decide you're going to play for an afternoon and see what happens. That's a growth strategy a major technology company uses to boost creativity—they give their engineering team 24 hours every quarter to work on their own projects and see what happens (which is why we now have Post Its, I do believe—the glue for Post Its was originally a failed batch of glue meant for aerospace and the formula sat for about five years until someone started playing with it and, seven years after that, Post Its were born.)

At any rate, being in Integrity leads to greater creativity and giving your creativity a structure of some sort creates the space for something new to emerge. (Kinda makes you want to go create something now, doesn't it?) ;+)

Life Purpose

Webster's Definition of Congruence: *"Congruence is the quality or state of agreeing or coinciding, a state achieved by coming together, the state of agreement."*

When you are living in Integrity with who you are here to be and the unique purpose you are to fulfill, your life has meaning and generates a deep sense of contentment within. Every decision you make defines you and makes you who you are—including how on track you are with your individual life purpose.

Life purpose is not found in a job or from something someone else says you are to do. Instead, it is what pulls you forward naturally—the thing that may seem too easy because you are usually doing it in some form consistently throughout your life.

Being aligned with your life purpose is one of the ultimate hallmarks of success because it will give you Energy, melt obstacles, and create opportunities without effort.

Conversely, when you are not in Integrity with your life purpose, your work feels like, well, work! You are not as interested as you could be, get side-tracked by challenges and distractions, and do not go the extra mile in how you show up for projects.

In this case, the best thing you can do is take some time to consider how you feel when you know you are aligned with something (usually that means happy, light and optimistic). When you have that feeling in mind, think about your life and the times you've felt that feeling—especially when working. That will give you a new approach to find clues about how your life purpose has expressed itself in the past so you can find new ways to express it going forward.

All in all, this is a good time to get into Integrity with yourself on all levels of your existence. Know that when you do, some people might not be happy. That's because they know you as they do and your shift will force them to shift to stay in relationship with you. If they are meant to be in your life going forward, that will happen with your mutual intention. And if not, you will need to choose between releasing them OR staying smaller than you were designed to be in this lifetime.

To clarify what it means to 'know' something... when you 'know' something, it means feeling the certainty of something with the same degree of knowingness as you know you are breathing. Stay firm in your vision, feel the power of internal and self-directed confidence, and give yourself the freedom to act in alignment with what you know to be true for you.

In summarizing the I in the GEENI System, sit and reflect on how Integrity is present in your life and business. This requires just a few minutes of your time, and it may be helpful to journal or doodle or diagram what comes up in your self-dialogue.

- Is your business in Integrity with your purpose and passion? Does it feel positive and abundant?
- Do you have personal habits that keep you out of Integrity?
- Do you check in with the Integrity of a project before proceeding to make sure it's a good/right fit?
- Are your boundaries in Integrity for both yourself and your business?
- For a challenge facing you now, are you handling it with Integrity?
- Are you using conscious language when communicating with others and in your marketing to be in Integrity with what you really want to say?

- Do you notice when you, your business or others are out of Integrity? How do you handle that?
- How do people respond to your presence when you walk into a room? By being aware, you can determine if they feel you are in Integrity with them or not.
- Is there anything you know right now that you need to handle or act on to be in greater Integrity? If yes, what is your plan to follow through?
- Is a wardrobe or image upgrade needed to be in greater Integrity with your business persona?
- Are your conversations in Integrity with what you mean? Do you follow through on what you say?
- When things do not flow, do you take ownership of what you can do to facilitate Integrity? Are you comfortable releasing what you can't control because you know you have shown up in Integrity?
- What happens when you proceed in a project or relationship where you know something is out of Integrity? How do you handle it?
- Where do you currently have Integrity in your life or business that you may have overlooked and want to acknowledge?
- In what ways can you use your Integrity to show up more powerfully and maximize positive results?
- Do you honor the highest vibration possible through Integrity in every moment? (This is not so easy... if you are achieving 80%, you are doing well!)

Your Integrity really is everything in achieving your dreams and goals. By seeing where you are in (and out of) Integrity, you can gain clarity and make conscious choices for next-step actions.

Summary and Next Steps

If you made it this far reading this book, you are ready for something new and different in expressing who you are with what you're doing and how you're showing up in the world. It's about creating success by your definition, on your terms. It's about integrating your intuition with your logic to get a bigger picture and create new possibilities.

Choices can hold you back but chances can set you free. Take a chance on gaining new freedom through clarity, bypassing your logical mind, and activating your intuitive potential by using the GEENI System regularly.

Thoughts are powerful and the unconscious mind is their obedient servant. Like the Genie in Aladdin's lamp, the unconscious mind says, *"Your wish is my command."* It begins to create whatever you think about... or worry about, which is a negative use of imagination.

Don't confuse your mind by staying on track one day and lapsing into doubt or negativity the next. Give your Genie-mind clear instructions, and you will soon be living your new mindset. To shape your future, you need to be ready and able to shape your mindset. You can get out of your own way by listening to your best source of personal information—your intuition.

Your inner guide is just waiting for you to ask a good question, as you now know. You can directly access the source that's always with you—your intuition—when you know what that means on a practical level.

Even more, when you start living from your inside out, you will be making wiser decisions based on what's true for you. You do risk not fitting into what other people think of as "normal" anymore... but the reward is you will be living from your personal clarity.

When you want to start getting through your life lessons faster, make decisions more clearly, and take more focused action to get you where you want to go, it's time to start working with your GEENI. Because, in the end, you are your own genie. (I know—it sounds schmaltzy... but it's true!) ;+)

In closing, please visit my website and let me know what you need to understand more about activating your intuitive potential so you can gain perfect clarity for your business, experience more freedom, and make a bigger difference in the world.

If this seems too good to be true for you, remember, "When the student is ready, the master appears." That is, when you are ready to learn something or take new action, the resources you need to support you in that new direction will show up. That just happened here through this book.

Now that you have the GEENI System, use it! What's waiting for you is the clarity you want for your life and business.

Use the GEENI to be your genie and please keep me posted on what happens for you and your business. I look forward to celebrating with you.

~ Lynn

P.S.: Be sure to post a comment about how much you like the GEENI System and/or if this brought up questions for you, please share them on my **Facebook page**. I'd love to know! (Who knows? You may inspire my next book!) :+)

The People Who Get the Greatest Value from My Work

My clients are typically people who are ready for BIG change. They are conscious truth-seekers who are ready to GO for it and finally 'arrive' where they want to be in life and business. Whatever the risk or the sacrifice, they know they are here for a purpose and to live from that place is so amazing it's just painful to live anywhere else. These people respect Energy. They 'get' the subtle but powerful influences that shape our lives. They are ready to work with someone (me) who can help them tap that limitless power to live even beyond their wildest imagination. They want more peak experiences. And they want who they really are—their most essential self—to be the compass and inspiration for their everyday life.

My would-be clients need to know every aspect of their life will be touched by our work together. It's upsetting and thrilling and not to be messed with lightly because their B.S. (Belief Systems) will be upgraded. When they are ready for that, great! When they are not ready, or if the fear of their own potential stops them before they start, then we are probably not a match.

At the same time, if they have tried on their own and failed but are still going, still seeing there is 'more' for them, then they have the heart to do this work and I want to work with them.

By the way, my goal is to work myself out of my work with clients. This is about jumpstarting their 'new normal' and making sure they have access to what they need to live their extraordinary and precious life.

Maybe you know it's time for you to take your life and business to the next level but have not yet figured out what that means or how to do it. Traditional marketing would have you do studies and surveys, test market your offers, and analyze results. That's just not how I work—for me, it's about who you are being through your business. Once that gets lined up with your truth, everything else will fall into line.

I believe business is our highest calling made manifest through service. When you are aligned with that, money is a by-product of being who you are.

If you've worked with me before, you'll recognize the value of my work. If you haven't yet worked with me, you need to know I'm a rich content teacher who is bi-lingual—I speak the language of business and the language of spirit.

The sweet spot of my work is to reveal that which was previously hidden to you about your path to success and abundance. I have been gifted with strong intuition and with being a high communicator.

On a personal note, it is my heart's desire and sacred responsibility to support you in living your best life in every way. It's not a destination but a daily experience. When it feels right, reach out and let me know of your interest in working together.

When you feel clear, strong, happy, healthy and free, congratulations—you've arrived.

FREE Insights

If you want to learn more about the
New Entrepreneur to see if you are one, go to:

https://lynnscheurell.com/defining-new-entrepreneur/

About Lynn Scheurell

Lynn's path to becoming an intuitive started early. At age 6, she was seeing people who had crossed over, like her Uncle Eddie in his zoot suit the night he passed.

At age 13, she was hanging with her two best friends in the front yard talking about what it would be like when they were old—like 30. She predicted one would be married with children and the other a corporate New York go-getter—both turned out to be true. At 17, she heard the words 'you are here to actualize potential' and *knew* that was her life purpose.

By 22, she was on the entrepreneurial path. In fact, she was one of the original phone psychics back in the day (before it was popular to have a psychic on speed dial).

For Lynn, using her intuition in business is sacred because it is about serving others to help them have a better life by their own definition—the money is a by-product of doing good work. What lights her up about this work is seeing people's lives change instantly. It is typical for people to change lifelong beliefs within the first 60 minutes as a result of new and compelling clarity.

Lynn has always been fascinated by human development. She says, "*I just knew what I knew... I was an intuitive catalyst for people to have more of what they wanted before personal coaching was even a glimmer of an industry.*"

Lynn Scheurell's philosophy is that all events and outcomes are connected to universal consciousness.

When you know how to strategically access and apply your innate and Natural Intelligence within that framework, you are able to shift perspective and make an instant impact to get the results you want.

She further believes that, once you have the clarity to observe your own power through your own actions, your patterns and your Environment, you give yourself access to the power you have to punch holes in your personal myths and limitations to create new results.

Today, her clients report that Lynn's intuitive gift has given them insight and courage to make even the toughest decisions easier—everything from getting a divorce to investing in major property deals to finding their life purpose to systematically monetizing what they know.

Having worked with thousands of people at this point, her clients have come from a variety of backgrounds to live their dreams and personal truths through clarity.

At the time of this printing, Lynn lives in the foothills of Tucson, Arizona with her four-legged beloved soulmate, Luna.

Lynn can be reached at her personal website at:

LynnScheurell.com.

Twitter: **@LynnScheurell**
Facebook: **/MyCreativeCatalyst** (Fan Page)
LinkedIn: **linkedin.com/in/lynnscheurell/**
Instagram: **instagram.com/lynnscheurell/**

Book Lynn Scheurell to Speak

Book Lynn Scheurell as your Speaker to Make Your Event Inspirational, Motivational, Entertaining and Memorable!

Lynn Scheurell has been teaching and inspiring entrepreneurs, business owners, experts, consultants, and coaches to access and use their wisdom as the pathway to business growth. Likewise, their business can be the modality through which they gain self-mastery.

Her origin story includes growing up as a sensitive ahead of her time in Milwaukee, WI, working as one of the original phone psychics back in the day (because there were no other "mainstream" ways to use intuition!) and becoming a professional Catalyst before it was cool. After taking an unconventional approach through building businesses for herself and her clients, Lynn can share relevant, actionable strategies to activate intuitive potential and accelerate results—even if people don't believe they have an intuitive bone in their bodies.

Her unique style is warm, personal, positive, and inspiring. She empowers and entertains audiences while giving them the tools and guidance they need and want to get beyond their logical limitations into intuitive clarity so they can accelerate fresh results in their businesses.

For more info and to book Lynn to speak at your next event, please visit **lynnscheurell.com/book-lynn/**.

Other Books by Lynn Scheurell

Here I am at a book signing—fun! :+)

The Energy of Money: How to Understand and Quantum Leap Your Relationship with Money Using Metaphysical Insights

Feng Shui for Entrepreneurs: Harnessing the Power of Your Environment for Business Success

Perspectives: Digital Transformation Through the Lens of Strategic Marketing

Defining Your Purposeful Prosperity Path: How to Make Opportunities, a Business Model and a Living from Your Wisdom

One Last Thing

If you enjoyed this book or found it useful, I'd be grateful if you'd post a short review on Amazon. Your support really does make a difference. I read all the reviews personally so I can get your feedback and make this book even better.

If you'd like to leave a review, then all you need to do is click the review link on this book's page on Amazon here:

GEENIBook.com

Thanks again for your support!

www.ingramcontent.com/pod-product-compliance
Lightning Source LLC
Chambersburg PA
CBHW072052290426
44110CB00014B/1651